Prayers of Surrender

72 Stories from the Heart

compiled by
Carol Broadbooks

*To the wonderful leaders with
whom I have served and to the
children for whom we pray*

TABLE OF CONTENTS

FOREWORD

One of the greatest privileges and joys I have had in the last 25 years is to have served alongside the authors of the devotionals you are about to read. I saw God at work in them as they served with their spouses to further the Kingdom through the Church of the Nazarene in the United States and Canada.

Each time we gathered together, our most precious times were when I heard them pray out to God for their families, their spouses, and the ministry to which God had called them. I pray that as you read their words and prayers of surrender, you will be encouraged to be steadfast in your own prayers.

Let us keep our eyes lifted up to the One who hears and answers our prayers.

"Continue earnestly in prayer, being vigilant in it with thanksgiving."
Colossians 4:2

ReJOYcing in answered prayer,

Prayers Do Prevail

Becky Armstrong
Illinois District

"Jesus Christ is the same yesterday and today and forever."
HEBREWS 13:8

During the night as I sat rocking one of my grandsons who was not feeling well, I prayed for him. I rocked and prayed, embracing the time and thanking God for the privilege of getting to spend those special moments with him. At the same time, I was a little uneasy, being aware of the virus that is changing all our lives, and I continued praying for his health.

Those thoughts and prayers led to praying for the other grandchildren and my children, sharing with God specific praises and concerns for each one. God then began reminding me of times He had answered my prayers.

One evening, one of our sons walked in and tossed a speeding ticket at me saying, "Well, your prayers have been answered." I had not prayed he would get a ticket, but I had prayed God would slow him down without anyone getting hurt.

One of our children was rather rambunctious and daring. I often prayed God would channel that energy into something positive for the Lord. As an adult, he has stepped out in faith to begin an organic church in a gym called CrossFit RWOL (Restoring Wholeness of Life).

When our daughter was small, she hid behind me when others spoke to her. She did not want to stay away from home for any reason, and going to school was a challenge. I understood her fears and prayed about the situation often. Following the suggestion to send something of mine with her every day, I sent a necklace, which helped. Today that young woman is an assistant principal. God has guided her into a position to encourage parents and help many children.

I have prayed for wisdom to know how to help one of my children who struggled academically, for the healing of broken bones and broken hearts, how to parent and grandparent, and how to be a parent of adult children. I now pray for help in knowing how to be a long distance parent or grandparent, and I always ask God to please help them all to have a relationship with Him.

And God says to me, "I am here. I am available. I care. I am working. I am the same today as I was when your children were young and when you were young. I am the same One who raised people from the dead, healed the sick, and forgave the woman at the well. I am the same yesterday, today, and forever."

Whatever fears, concerns, or joys we have, let us talk with God about them.

Prayer

Father, thank You for being available all the time and allowing us to bring whatever concerns we have to You. Thank You for caring about all of our children and grandchildren even more than we do. You know their needs and wants and everything that concerns them. God, please continue to take care of our children.

Where Does My Help Come From?

Judy Askren
South Arkansas District

"I lift up my eyes to the mountains—where does my help come from?
My help comes from the LORD, the Maker of heaven and earth."
PSALM 121:1-2

"Hello?"

When I replaced the phone receiver after the conversation ended, I was sick to my stomach and shaky. This was not what I had planned. I could feel the sweat on my forehead; my heart started racing. I needed to talk with my husband; surely, he would feel the same as me!

I burst into his office and told him the news. Our 16-year-old daughter had been selected to be a page for the House of Representatives in D.C., an entire continent away from us. And she needed to be there in five weeks. I could feel the panic bubbling up inside of me. I didn't see how this could be a good thing for her spiritually. When I shared this with my husband, he just shook his head and said, "Of course she's going! God has given her a great opportunity!" I didn't tell him I only agreed to let her apply because I didn't think she would be selected.

In the weeks leading up to her departure, I was able to push the panic down—mostly. We went to D.C. and got her settled in the dorm and met teachers and the director of the program while praying over our child the whole time. After we returned home, the worry set in. There were rules to guard her safety, but who was guarding my daughter spiritually? One of the assistant directors of their dorm transported anyone who wanted to attend a church in the area, and I am still grateful to God for His providence. But who was guarding my daughter's every encounter?

Each night when I laid my head on my pillow, the panic would push up again and I would cry out to God to protect her from evil. I had a hard time sleeping. Worry was constant. I could feel myself changing.

The Lord was faithful and graciously gave me some time. After weeks and months of hearing my pleas, He very firmly spoke to me in the midst of one of my outbursts. "Judy, do you trust Me?" "Of course, Lord," I replied. "No. Do you TRUST Me?" "Of course I do." "Do you trust Me with your salvation?" "Yes, completely." "But you don't trust Me with your child?" Complete silence.

I was horrified to realize that I didn't. I had allowed the choking worry to creep into my prayer life, my thought life, my relationship with my Savior. I was ashamed and knew my behavior had to change. My faith needed to plant itself deeply in my thought life.

I made a conscious decision to hand over all my worry and my fears to my Savior, who knows my daughter so much better than I do. It is a deliberate act of my will each day to entrust my children to the Creator. Whenever I start to slip up, His Holy Spirit reminds me that I can rest in His care and place my children in His hands. He is faithful! In all things.

Prayer

Father, thank You for Your faithfulness to us even when we aren't faithful to You. You are not only Creator and Savior but You are Comforter and Sustainer, an ever-present help in times of trouble. Thank You for convicting us and for not leaving us where we are today but encouraging us to be the people You have called us to be. We pray for our families in this moment, that Your Holy Spirit would continue to work in their lives and watch over them.

The Appetite-Denying Discipline

Jolyne Bartley
Northwest Indiana District

"When you practice some appetite-denying discipline to
better concentrate on God, don't make a production out of
it. It might turn you into a small-time celebrity but it won't
make you a saint. If you 'go into training' inwardly, act normal
outwardly. Shampoo and comb your hair, brush your teeth, wash
your face. God doesn't require attention-getting devices. He
won't overlook what you are doing; he'll reward you well."
MATTHEW 6:16-18 (MSG)

Early on in our marriage, Dave and I decided that we would wait to
start our family until he graduated from seminary. After his graduation,
we anticipated a positive pregnancy test, but that wasn't the journey our
lives took. We rejoiced when our friends became easily pregnant, all the
while wondering when it would be our turn to share the good news.
After many years of struggle, we both went to doctors and found out
that nothing seemed to be the problem. We were thankful to be healthy
but stumped as to why we couldn't conceive. After talking with our doctors, our next steps toward parenthood would involve a huge financial
obligation. Between my teaching salary and Dave's pastoral income,
we knew our budget couldn't stretch that far. We had been married 10
years and we were at a place of desperation, disappointment, and total
reliance on God to work a miracle.

After much conversation about our next course of action, Dave and
I vowed to privately pray and fast one day a week in hopes of getting pregnant. On the same day each week, we kept our commitment
and fervently prayed for God's will to be done, even if it meant that
we would be barren. These weeks were spent learning to tune out the

distractions, deepening our commitment to Christ, and really grappling with what total surrender to His plans might mean. I needed to come to a place where His will was done, not mine. It is a place that I still often need to come to Him.

Just two months later, we found out the exciting news that we were expecting our first child! We were completely overjoyed and marveled at the work that only God could do. It was such a blessing to be able to share our joy and our journey with our church congregation. Dave has had the opportunity to share and preach about God's call for us to pray and fast over our pregnancy. We quickly learned that the struggle we faced allowed us to be empathetic to those struggling with infertility while also encouraging those just beginning the discipline of prayer and fasting.

Since the birth of our first child, we have gone to God with prayer and private times of "denying our appetites to concentrate on God" on many occasions and have seen His miracles performed. We have fasted and prayed over our four children and our parents' health concerns. On a district level, we've used the practice of prayer and fasting to intercede for a local church in crisis, the heavy loss of a minister's credential, pastoral marriages in jeopardy, and parsonage children searching for hope. God can do amazing things when our focus is solely on Him and His provisions. We have been blessed to witness His miracles. I have learned that no prayer is too big, nor any request too small. If it matters to you and me, it matters to our Father.

Prayer

Dear Jesus, thank You for the discipline and gift of prayer and fasting. Lord, our lives are dedicated to the ministry of Your gospel. Teach us, Father, to know when to use prayer and fasting in the many needs we face. Our DS families are hurting, and our district pastoral families are facing discouragement. May we be faithful in praying for the needs of our people and may we be burdened to fast when You lay that on our heart. Thank You for Your faithfulness in providing exactly what we need in the situations we encounter. In Jesus' name, amen.

Joy in the Midst of Heartache

Debi Berry
Central Gulf Coast District

"Praise the Lord! For he has heard my cry for mercy. The
Lord is my strength and shield. I trust him with all my
heart. He helps me, and my heart is filled with joy."
PSALM 28:6-7 (NLT)

When we least expect, times of discouragement come our way. These unwelcomed interruptions can be devastating. We need to be prepared to overcome these paralyzing feelings. Satan's resolve is to cause believers—especially ministry folk—to lose their focus, passion, and motivation, and his scheme is to bring personally painful things our way. These distractions can overwhelm, discourage, and sometimes even crush us, ultimately distracting us from ministry. Satan knows that the most poignant way to do this is through their family, especially their children. When our kids hurt, we hurt more and often go into alarm mode—not a pretty sight always! We cannot effectively serve God when we are focused on life's distractions and disappointments.

It takes real strength and wherewithal to fight against the evil one. With God's help, we can withstand and combat the fiery attacks and harassment of the devil.

The older I get, the more determined I am to not allow Satan to get the better of me. I don't always win, but as I stand firm in my resolve, I overcome! As I cry for help, the Lord comes to my aid. When I recognize Satan's assault on my family and then call for help, I am shielded from the barbs of Satan and strengthened by God. I can truly say the JOY of the Lord is my strength!

So how can we remain JOYFUL when we are deeply heartsick? It is not easy! I have learned some ways to overcome sadness and overwhelming disappointment. I will share them using the acrostic JOYFUL:

J = JESUS loves our children more than we do—imagine that! That reality is both awesome and comforting! Every day, release your children and unsaved ones into God's hands (or re-release) them.

O = ONLY allow yourself 15 minutes a day to worry and fret over your child and then pray that God would continue to woo your child to Himself. Cling to scriptures of hope and songs of praise and comfort as a follow-up to your prayer.

Y = YIELD not! Determine to not allow the "joy robber" to steal your joy. Exercise your faith and stand firm.

F = FIND a hobby or ministry of encouragement to fill your days and get your focus off yourself and your heartaches. As I once heard Luci Swindoll say, "Don't sit, soak, and sour."

U = UNDERSTAND the tactics of the enemy. Cut him off at the pass! Recognize the evil one's plots.

L = LASTLY, remain hopeful, believing that God knows all about your heartaches, your child's waywardness, the situation, and is at work—even if you can't see Him working. Trust Him to do His work in HIS time.

When feelings of sadness, fear, or anxiety set in, I recognize the source and determine to not let Satan steal my joy. My prayer is that I will remain an overcomer as I trust God with all my heart in times of need. Corrie ten Boom said, "Joy runs deeper than despair." So, I choose joy!

Prayer

Heavenly Father, in times of heartache and worry, draw near. May Your strong arms of comfort envelop me and still my anxious thoughts. Restore my joy and grant me peace, as I trust You. I praise You for Your loving kindness and for being a mender of hearts!

Unconditional Love for Our Children

Susanne Blake
Indianapolis District

"Dear friends, since God so loved us,
we also ought to love one another."
1 JOHN 4:11

Christ's unconditional love for us models how we can love and pray for our children. We cannot beat ourselves up over the past by saying, "What if…" or "If only…" The truth is that our children have free will. They must decide for themselves to serve God. The heartbreaking question we ask at times is "Where did I go wrong?" The fact is that yes, we were not perfect parents, but we cannot control our children's decisions. Most of us tried to make every effort for our kids to be influenced by godly people and grow up listening to the Gospel message. We thought that those experiences would make them Christians. Yet salvation through Christ still comes down to a personal decision.

I want to give unconditional love to my child regardless of where he is spiritually. My desire is to love him like Christ loves me.

I pray the Holy Spirit will use life experiences to lead my child into a relationship with Christ.

Let my prayer be "Holy Spirit, have Your way in reaching my child."

So let us not give up but keep diligently praying, knowing the Holy Spirit will work in ways we cannot. God does love our children unconditionally.

Prayer

In my time with You, You remind me that I did many things right in raising my child. Yet the voice inside me may still say that I did not convince my child that following You was a great way to live. I continue to rest in the fact that my prayers are making a difference even though I do not see changes. I love my child, but You love him even more. Help me trust You in faith and believe that You have heard my prayers, You have seen my tears, and You will answer. Amen.

Beyond Forgiveness

Donna Bond
Kansas District

"Be ye kind one to another, tenderhearted, forgiving one
another, even as God for Christ's sake hath forgiven you."
EPHESIANS 4:32 (KJV)

We had a very special friend in one of the churches we pastored. His name was Sammy. Sammy was a middle-aged special needs man that endeared himself to everyone, and especially to this pastoral family. His birthday was coming up and we had told him that on Sunday we would take him to his favorite place to eat, Cracker Barrel! Well, Sunday came and we forgot all about taking Sammy to Cracker Barrel until late that Sunday evening. We felt terrible. The next Sunday, Jim went up to Sammy and asked for forgiveness. With a big, toothy smile, Sammy said, "It's okay. I forgave you when it happened." Needless to say, we took him out to Cracker Barrel that Sunday.

As a district superintendent's wife, I travel all across Kansas, meeting many wonderful laymen and pastors. I sit in on board meetings, pastoral reviews, church celebrations, and special events. Because of my proximity to the district superintendent (my husband), I also hear many unpleasant conversations among church members and pastors. I am sure you do, too. People get offended and either leave the church or stay and hold a grudge. It is hard to hear and watch such situations.

I have become keenly aware of the need for God's people to put into practice the Bible verse that was quoted to me many times while growing up: "And be ye kind one to another, tenderhearted, forgiving one another, even as God for Christ's sake hath forgiven you" Ephesians 4:32 (KJV). I think most of us have the being kind to each other mastered, but I think forgiving one another is something we have come to think of as optional in our spiritual journeys. Or maybe we do forgive but we secretly carry a grudge (which makes me question whether forgiveness really took place).

Have you ever wondered why people go to the altar, pray for the ability to forgive, and in just a short time, they are right back again having the same problems with bitterness, anger, and hypersensitivity, asking for help? Maybe you are one of these people. You have been hurt by friends, or worse, family. We have forgiven them, but the feelings of bitterness and anger just keep coming back to us. The reason for this is that we are not doing what God instructs us to do. Though God tells us to forgive others, He wants us to go beyond forgiveness to bless and speak well of them. "Love your enemies, do good to those who hate you, bless those who curse you, pray for those who mistreat you" (Luke 6:27-28). Jesus says we are not only to forgive but also to do good, bless, and pray for those that hurt us. Those are difficult words.

We may wrongly think we are asking God for their physical or material blessings. The truth is we are praying for them to be blessed spiritually—to bring truth and revelation to them about their attitude and behavior so they will be willing to repent and be freed from their sins.

Why spend your life angry at people? Release them. Let the offense go, and have the same attitude Jesus had toward His enemies. You will experience wonderful freedom, and God will show Himself strong as your vindicator. The Lord wants us to live an unbelievably blessed life through Him. Don't let those blessings be hindered by living in bitterness and resentment toward others.

Prayer

Heavenly Father, thank You for Your comforting, yet correcting Word that shows me how to live a victorious life. Thank You for Your forgiveness and unconditional love. Bring to mind any unforgiveness, bitter thoughts, or grudges that I am holding. I release these to You this day. I pray for those who have hurt me (either intentionally or unintentionally); may You bless them in all ways, but especially spiritually. Thank You for Your answered prayer, Jesus. Amen.

Mom's Missionary Prayers

Diane Falvo Bowser
Mid-Atlantic District

"And pray in the Spirit on all occasions with all kinds of
prayers and requests. With this in mind, be alert and
always keep on praying for all the Lord's people."
EPHESIANS 6:18

There was a stop sign on the way to my son's high school. He always knew what happened when we reached that point. I have often thought about that place in the road, a place where two streets intersect, a place where people going in different directions meet. It symbolizes one's journey, a spiritual journey.

Over the years, the stop sign has probably been replaced with a round-about designed to keep traffic moving. We need stop signs along the way. They help reevaluate and reframe the direction we are heading to in life.

Our drive to school always involved conversation until we reached that four-way stop. This sign meant we stopped to pray. We prayed until we reached the front of the school building. There were times I was not finished praying and we continued with our eyes wide open as students passed by the car. My son Brandon called it "mom's missionary prayers."

"Mom's missionary prayers" continued throughout our kids' college years. Although the roads traveled were across state lines, "mom's missionary prayers" never stopped. Ashley and Brandon worked at a Salvation Army camp in Sharon, Massachusetts. Over the years, Camp Wonderland has been a great influence on thousands of Boston's inner-city children. Many of them arrive with nothing but the clothes on their back. After returning from one of his summers working at Camp Wonderland, he announced, "When I graduate from college, I am going back to Boston to teach the kids I worked with." And that is exactly what he did!

We never know how God is going to work and speak into the lives of our children. We don't know what or who God chooses to use to get our children's attention. As I have prayed for my children, God has sent me many reassuring signs that He is speaking. Brandon has been teaching in Boston for eight years. He has sent me pictures of a church van sitting in front of his school with the Church of the Nazarene's Spanish logo on its side panel.

Somewhere there are Nazarene "missionaries" in his school. On one particular day, a student said, "Mr. Bowser, do you believe in God?" The student added, "I am going to pray for you." "Mom's missionary prayers" are being answered.

Brandon is a Boston pedicab driver during the summer tourist months. Several summers ago, he sent a picture with his arm around two people I did not recognize. He learned in conversation that they were retired missionaries. His message accompanying the picture read, "missionaries ride free."

Boston is a special place to our family. Graduating from ENC, we spent many years up and down the streets of this beautiful, historic city. Going places with Brandon is so much fun because he seems to know everyone. In a recent run for Boston City Council, he mingled with those throughout the community he loves.

Recently, while visiting him in Boston, we ate a delicious dinner together before heading home. He continued ordering food, far more than we could ever eat in one meal.

After leaving the restaurant, he said to us, "Wait here." While waiting, we saw Jesus reflected in him as he stooped down to look into the eyes of two unkempt runaway teens and their dog. Brandon said something to each of them while handing them the take-out bags of food from the restaurant. When he returned to where we had been waiting, we asked, "What did you say to them?" He responded compassionately, "I told them, 'Call your parents and let them know where you are.'"

Years have passed and "mom's missionary prayers" are still being prayed daily. I received a text message from Brandon recently on his final day of a four-week trip to India. It read, "I woke in my hotel room to the sound of a church group singing, 'then sings my soul, my Savior God to thee.'" Only God orchestrates moments like this.

Prayer

Thank You Lord, for the opportunity to serve You, wherever You place us. Continue to put us in the path of those that need to see You, above their circumstances. Lord, we want to be sensitive people; sensitive to the many and varied needs of those we interact with. Take us to a deeper place through the power of the Holy Spirit. Strengthen and stretch us. Keep us alert to the needs of those in front of us. Help us to see people as You see them. Lead us to those we have intentionally or unintentionally looked past, walked around, ignored. Help us love as You love. May it be so. Amen.

Praying through Change

Tammi Brown
North Central Ohio District

"Jesus Christ is the same yesterday and today and forever."
HEBREWS 13:8

Our youngest child always said, "That will take a long time," when we asked him to wait for something as a toddler. As his high school graduation approaches, I've been thinking how different his perspective of time is from ours. The reality is that this has gone by way too fast!

Although it is fast, it seems at times we are slow in learning how to adapt as a parent. Now that our children are adults, we are discovering that you never stop being a parent, you just have to learn how to parent and pray differently.

When the children were young, we prayed for their schoolwork, their "boo-boos," and family and friends every night. In our quiet time as parents, we asked God to help them know that He could be trusted. We remember the excitement of seeing our oldest raise her hands in worship for the first time and believing that because of her action, we must be on the right track.

In the teenage years, you are praying for safety as they drive cars and asking God to keep them pure and help them avoid temptation. In our quiet time, we asked God to help them develop a heart of love for Him. Parents experience many emotional swings in these years. You experience the joy of their strengthened relationship with Christ after Nazarene Youth Conference only to experience devastation a short time later when you learn of a relationship with a boy that is leading your daughter far away from Christ.

As they enter their college years, you start to believe you have a handle on how to pray for them when everything changes again. You pray for their decisions and their potential spouse, asking God to help them learn to stand on their own two feet. You discover that their faith doesn't depend on their parents. You struggle with your words as you try to guide them instead of telling them what to do. You pray and ask God how to parent, knowing that you are learning new skills as you pray them into adulthood. You experience your first college graduate who hugs your neck on graduation day to tell you how thankful they were that you believed in them.

Finally, the adult years. You pray for their employment and the career they are pursuing. You pray that they will have the right values for their lives and set the right priorities. You pray for their finances and ask God to help them understand what it means to be a faithful steward. As their life and careers progress, you communicate less than you have at the other stages. You worry about them, but at the same time, they tell you that they have found a church and LOVE going there. You learn to give them advice when they ask for it, although sometimes if you are honest, you wish they needed you a little more.

As you pray, God reveals something to you about yourself, your children, and His character. First, life is changing faster than you can keep up with as a parent. Second, life is changing faster than your child can keep up with as well. Third, God hasn't changed at all. The same God you entrusted your life to and the lives of your children to when they were born is the same God that you are speaking with today. He is love, and He loves your children. You breathe a sigh of relief to realize that because He has not changed, your trust has never been in vain. Parents and children change, but He does not!

Not long ago, I saw something that read, "Pray so BIG and so OFTEN that when God meets you at the Heaven's Gate, He says with a SMILE, 'Kid, you kept Me VERY busy.'" May this be true in our prayers for our children.

Prayer

Heavenly Father, thank You for the gift of parenthood. Thank You for the ability to come before Your throne to pray for our children. No matter what stage of life they or we are in, let us NEVER forget that You never change. Help us to be still when we need to be and to be Your voice to our children when we need to be as well. In Your precious name we pray, amen.

Big or Small, He Is in It All

Christi Busic
General Superintendent Spouse

"Truly I tell you, whatever you bind on earth will be bound in heaven,
and whatever you loose on earth will be loosed in heaven."
MATTHEW 18:18

We have three children. We have prayed endless prayers over them through the years. I have learned a few things, and yet many things remain a mystery. However, one thing that is not a mystery is that the size of the need does not seem to be an issue for God. He asks us to come to Him with all our concerns.

We have a child that struggled with change for many reasons. When this child entered ninth grade, we changed schools—from a big, overwhelming situation to a small, private setting. Just for the one child. It was one of our best decisions. Our child became more involved, flourished, tried things for the first time, and made many new friends. But change was coming again.

Being in ministry, you understand when you feel that God may be changing your future. I knew my child. I knew this would be hard, especially after having such a great school year—but I trusted God. I began praying specifically for this child. I asked God to prepare their heart, because I knew it would be hard. I prayed for several months, and then we received the call to move from Kansas City to Bethany, Oklahoma. When the time came to tell the children, it was this child who was the most excited. I may have had a shocked expression, but I knew God had answered my prayer. Bethany became a place of healing and untold blessings.

Our next child was making a life partner decision. David and I really struggled with this decision. We could see the problems and dangers ahead, but we faced a wall of determination. A week before the wedding, a prayer warrior gave us a message from God. It said many things, including to trust Him. The next five and a half years were some of the hardest we have ever faced as we watched our child disappear before our eyes. This once strong, vibrant, confident child became a shadow of their self. I may have cried every week of those years. The prayers became hard because we did not know what to do. Nevertheless, He answered those prayers over time. Through a painful divorce, counseling, a loving family, and hosts of friends, our child returned and is now married to someone who truly cherishes them. We could not be more grateful.

The first story may seem smaller in perspective to the second, but the impact for each child was significant. I can only encourage you to keep praying for your child no matter the age. We know them so well. Who better to pray for them? This is my prayer for you: be encouraged. Don't give up. Trust in Him even when the storm rages.

Prayer

Lord, hear our prayers. They are many, but You care for each request. I believe in You to answer them in Your timing. Our children are gifts You have given to us, and we will honor those gifts by bringing them to Your throne. Hear us, Lord, as we cry out to You. Your love for us and our children is something we cannot fully fathom or grasp. We trust in You alone! Amen.

Prayer Anchored in Hope

Samantha Chambo
General Superintendent Spouse

"May the God of hope fill you with all joy and peace, as you trust in him,
so that you may overflow with hope by the power of the Holy Spirit."
ROMANS 15:13

Advent is a season of hope. Hope is the expectation or belief in the fulfillment of something desired and incorporates ideas of waiting and endurance. In the Bible, this hope is always based on the person and work of God.

My friend came to the Lord as a hopeless alcoholic, and God delivered her miraculously. However, a few months ago, after almost 10 years of sobriety, she phoned me. She said she has started to drink again and she was out of control. I went to see her and we prayed together. A few weeks later, I met her at an event. She was wearing big celebrity glasses as she walked up to me. I asked her how she was and she took off her glasses. I was shocked at what I saw. Her face was swollen and her eyes seemed glazed. She smelled of stale alcohol that testified to how she spent her Friday night, and there was just a sense of hopelessness and sorrow on her. I immediately opened my arms to her, without words, and we just stood there for a while, crying as I prayed for God to have mercy on her. That was a crisis moment for me because, at that point, I just could not see how God was going to do this. He saved her once, but can He do it again? I was praying for her, but the hopelessness came over me like a dark cloud.

I know we all have experienced a sense of hopelessness in some way. Illness, financial problems, loved ones caught in the grip of vicious addictions, and a host of other situations can lead to a feeling of hopelessness.

A wise man once said that hardship, difficulty, and despair is the fertile soil for hope. This is the meaning of hope in the Bible.

From the books of Genesis to Revelation, hope springs up in the face of seemingly impossible situations. It started in the Garden of Eden. Adam and Eve's disobedience plunged the whole creation into a hopeless situation. God made this promise: that He will raise up the seed of woman to crush the head of the serpent. This was a prophesy pointing to the coming of Jesus. This is also the message of Paul in the epistle to the Romans. He explains that God did not forget His promise to set all things right. God can still be trusted to fulfill His promise in spite of the apparent dominance of evil.

This Christmas season, we remember that the birth of Jesus Christ was God breaking into human history for our redemption. The Messiah has finally come to bring freedom and liberation and to reverse the consequences of sin. Jesus Christ is the root of Jesse (Isaiah 42:1-4, Romans 15:12), the expected king that we have been waiting for. And with the coming of Jesus, the kingdom of God has broken into the world.

This salvation is universal; it is for all of us. It is relevant to my situation in my little corner. Jesus Christ came to set all things right, and that is why we can have hope.

Prayer

May the God of hope fill you with all joy and peace, as you trust in Him, so that you may overflow with hope by the power of the Holy Spirit (Romans 15:13).

Faith, Not Fear!

Roxanna Cole
Nebraska District

"For God has not given us the spirit of fear;
but of power, and of love, and of a sound mind."
2 TIMOTHY 1:7

These have been trying, difficult days for people all around the world. When I think about it, I am not sure that a lot of us saw this COVID-19 pandemic coming—I sure didn't. One day you are going through daily routines and then, all of the sudden, life is turned upside down. Normal isn't normal anymore. Routines have been uprooted. We hear new words and phrases like social distancing, the new normal, unprecedented times, quarantine, and Zoom conferencing. I had never heard of Zoom before! What is that?

The pandemic has ushered in a lot of fear, but, as long as there is Jesus, there is hope! We do not need to live in fear in any situation we find ourselves in this life. Dan often reminds people when he is preaching that "whatever you're dealing with in your life, it hasn't caught God off-guard!" So true! COVID-19, or anything else for that matter, has not caught God off-guard! He is watching over us. We don't need to be fearful! Thank the good Lord!

The devil likes to bind us up in fear. He did that to the disciples after the Crucifixion. The Bible says, "On the evening of that first day of the week, when the disciples were together, with the doors locked for fear of the Jewish leaders, Jesus came and stood among them and said, 'Peace be with you!'" (John 20:19). That is what we need Jesus to do for us whenever we are afraid—walk into the room and hold His hand up and say, "Peace be with you!" I need that. We all need that! Every day of our lives, whether we are experiencing a pandemic or helping our kids and grandkids walk through difficult times, you name it; we just need Jesus to whisper in our ear "Peace be with you!"

Let's live in faith, not fear! Whatever happens in our lives or to our world, let's make the choice to stay faithful to Jesus and the job He has called us to do. "For we live by faith, not by sight!" (2 Corinthians 5:7). We're seeing a lot of scary things on the news these days—family and friends are losing their jobs, more than 300,000 people have died as a result of COVID-19, businesses are closing down, many of which will never reopen, families are in great crisis; the list goes on and on! We just need Jesus to speak peace into our hearts.

When our family was facing very scary, difficult times in the days following Dan's open-heart surgery (nearly six years ago, now) Jesus turned our fear to faith. It wasn't that we had lost our faith; we were just plain scared! We were close to losing Dan. God stepped in. He steered our fear back to faith. Jesus came in, raised His hand, and said, "Peace be with you!" Dan shares that as he was "coming back to himself," he felt Jesus speak to him and say, "I've got this!"

This is not a time for Christians to shrink back! This is the time for us to step up and let people know that "God's got this!" We choose faith over fear. The Bible says, "But we do not belong to those who shrink back and are destroyed, but to those who have faith and are saved" (Hebrews 10:39).

Prayer

Jesus, please help us to always choose faith over fear. Would You step into our lives and whisper in our ears and to our hearts, "Peace be with you!" Jesus, would You do that in our country and in our world today? Somehow, step into this chaos and whisper "Peace be with you" to many in our lives who desperately need to hear it. Help them and us to see the need to trade fear for faith! Amen.

Time

Ruth Collins
Canada Atlantic District

"Rejoice always, pray continually, give thanks in all
circumstances; for this is God's will for you in Christ Jesus."
1 THESSALONIANS 5:16-18

I was reminded the other day of an "old song" by Larnelle Harris about God missing His time with us. I was rushing through my devotions, thinking of all I needed to accomplish that day—events and plans for the district, my job, connecting with family and friends, my grown children, meetings that were coming up—and then it hit me. Can you imagine showing up late for an important meeting? Or getting to an important meeting and then not paying attention to the leader or speaker? We would never do that here on earth, but that was exactly what I was doing with my devotional and prayer time. My most important meeting of each day is with God, and I was treating Him and my time with Him with less respect than I would a mere mortal!

I stopped and cleared my mind and prayed for forgiveness and His presence. It was so sweet. His Holy Spirit met me and gave me the strength, wisdom, and message I needed! I cannot get through a day without His presence with me!

As I reflected on all the years of running with our children, doing church activities, work, and life, I wondered how often I had left God behind because I didn't take the time to be with Him first! It was a great reminder to me that no matter how busy life gets, God needs to be first in our time!

Prayer

Dear Father, we are so thankful for Your patience with us. When we get too busy with our own agenda, You patiently wait for us to take time to sit at Your feet and worship You! We love You and pray we will hear Your voice and find Your perfect will! Amen.

From Bones to Breath

Betty Cooper
Southwest Oklahoma District

"So I prophesied as I was commanded. And as I was prophesying, there was a noise, a rattling sound, and the bones came together, bone to bone. I looked, and tendons and flesh appeared on them and skin covered them, but there was no breath in them.

"Then he said to me, 'Prophesy to the breath; prophesy, son of man, and say to it, "This is what the Sovereign Lord says: Come, breath, from the four winds and breathe into these slain, that they may live."' So I prophesied as he commanded me, and breath entered them; they came to life and stood up on their feet—a vast army."
EZEKIEL 37:7-10

The vision of the valley of dry bones in Ezekiel 37 is a favorite to so many of us. This scripture took on a new reality for us a few years ago.

In 1978, God blessed us with our answer to an intense prayer. Our lives changed forever with a knock on the door as a five-day-old, blonde-headed, blue-eyed, gorgeous baby girl was delivered to our house. We had less than 24-hours' notice but had prepared by buying (1) a baby rattle, (2) a baby bottle, and (3) an outfit for our new daughter to wear. I have no idea what we were thinking!

The days and weeks and months and years rolled by. She was a delight to our lives (except for one hormonal year when we didn't know if any of us would survive). When we moved to Brazil as missionaries for four years, she never complained, actually excelled and easily adapted to another culture as she completed all her high school years in this new environment. All was pretty much right in her world. Next came college graduation; she began her teaching career and then she met and married the "perfect guy" for her and moved only 3 ½ hours away. She gave birth to our first grandson.

All were roses, sunshine, and happiness until her husband walked out of the home, leaving her as a single mom with a 4-month-old baby. Her husband had decided he no longer wanted to be faithful to his marriage.

As her parents, we were hurt, devastated, and mad—really mad! The young man who had sat in Jim's office and declared his love for our precious daughter and vowed he would never hurt her now dared to walk away for another. He offered no financial support and left her with all their debt.

So, as all parents would do, we tried to help in any way we could. We were together every weekend to give her a little respite from baby care and listen as she shared her broken heart.

And then we accepted the assignment to move to the Southwest Oklahoma District. We left our only child and our only grandson and moved 1,400 miles away. The promise of visits at least every three months was not enough. All hope was gone. There was just no breath in her.

We began to prophesy—speak to the bones. We sent money, bought appliances, sent money, paid deposits, sent more money, bought cars, flew them to Oklahoma for multiple visits, bought clothes and shoes, and sent even more money. We did everything we knew to do. Speaking to bones was our attempt to fix it. We prayed; we cried out to God, asking Him for help and to fill her with hope again. I remember sitting in our living room with Jim and just crying because we felt so helpless and hopeless ourselves. We questioned if we were not praying for the right thing. We knew speaking to the bones helped. Ezekiel witnessed the bones connecting and being covered, but as the Scripture says, there was no life, no breath, no hope. Our daughter's life was still empty, void of faith and dreams.

And then we noticed that the Lord commanded Ezekiel to speak again but this time to the breath. In our desperation, we called out to the Spirit.

We called from the east, from the west, from the north, and from the south: "Holy Spirit, breathe into our daughter so she may live again."

Our faithful Lord heard our plea and over a period of a couple years, God moved in a beautiful way. We have seen those bones come to life and stand on their feet (v. 10). We know the Lord has spoken. We learned you could prophesy to the bones and there would still be no life, even though they stood upright, but when we called on the Spirit—from every possible direction—the breath entered those bones and gave real life, fresh faith, new hope, and restored dreams.

While we try to offer "fixes" for our children's struggles, let's remember, while helpful, that does not give life. Let's be sure to speak to the breath so our children know true life in Christ—fresh faith, new hope, and restored dreams. Let's continue to join together and call in every direction for the Spirit to breathe life in to our children. We are not without hope!

Prayer

Father, may we continue always to speak to the breath for our children—
especially those who are slain—so they may know fresh faith, new hope,
and restored dreams. Amen.

A Devotional for the Current Times

Rachel Crocker
General Superintendent Spouse

"He says, 'Be still, and know that I am God; I will be exalted among the nations, I will be exalted in the earth.'"
PSALM 46:10

Ever since I remember, my maternal grandmother taught my older brother and me to memorize scriptures. She would sit us down with paper and pencil to write down and memorize entire chapters of Scripture in Spanish, her native language. Our Spanish skills were not the best because we grew up speaking English in America, but grandma knew something that we didn't know at that time: "Train up a child in the way he should go, and when he is old, he will not depart from it." Spanish and the Bible were two things that I learned from my childhood!

Memorizing scriptures was something that I passed along to my kids, especially my oldest daughter. It was always great to work with her and see what my grandmother saw in us when we were growing up. These lessons from our childhood would end up shaping us and giving us the certainty of His assurance in hard times, uncertain times, times of illness and loss, and even now, in times of a global pandemic that has led so many to lose their jobs, their patience, their finances, and even their lives. It is for such a time as this that the lessons from Scripture have proven to be valuable and assuring.

I find assurance in the Word when I read that those who delight themselves in the Lord "shall be like a tree planted by the rivers of water, that brings forth its fruit in its season, whose leaf shall also not wither; and that whatever that they do shall prosper" (Psalm 1:3, NKJV)

I find renewal in the Word when I recall that the Lord is my guide (my shepherd) who takes me through peaceful, quiet moments and uses them to restore and renew my soul. In His Word, I find the comfort of knowing that even though I may walk through the valley of shadow of death, I will fear not because He has promised to be forever with me (Psalm 23:1-4)!

I find strength when I am reminded by His Word that no matter what happens on this troubled earth, even when it gets shaken, He is in the middle of it! He is our refuge! All that He requires of us is to "Be still and know that He is God." (Psalm 46:10). It is through circumstances like these that we can carve out some time to be still and experience the changing nature of stillness. Once you let yourself be still and listen to that sweet, small voice, you will never want to let go. And it is during this moment of stillness that you "will know" that He is whispering your name assuring you that "He is our refugee forever."

When I hear my child quoting Scripture in times of difficulty or expectation, I realize the beauty of what I learned from my grandmother—that God's Word helps me cling to the promises of the Lord who gives them and who sustains me.

Prayer

Thank You, Lord, for being my refuge and that I can find assurance in Your Word. Thank You for the blessings that were passed on to me and that I have been able to pass on to my children. Help me to always be still and know who You are as I listen to Your still, gentle voice. Amen.

Prodigal, Prayers, and Perplexing Problems

Cindy Crump
Southwest Indiana

"Then once again I fell prostrate before the Lord for
forty days and forty nights; I ate no bread and drank no
water, because of all the sin you had committed."
DEUTERONOMY 9:18

Our prodigal has a name, Matthew, which means, "gift from God." He certainly is! As a baby, Matthew would have to be woken up to eat—a stark contrast to his two-year-old sister, Melanie, who wanted to eat every two hours. As a young and busy pastor's wife, I thanked God daily for an "easy baby!"

"Lord make him wake up and make him hungry for you!"

Then as he grew, he wore an infectious smile, so much so that the people in our Okmulgee, Oklahoma, church called him "Smiley!" Thank God for this gift!

"Lord make him smile one day for you!"

Today, Matthew's smile, outgoing personality, and driven work ethic make him a great friend to many and a great employee! People who know him thank God for the gift of Matthew!

"Lord, may you call him to lead his friends and coworkers to you."

Matthew also has another area in which he is very strong—ego and pride. He has opinions, thoughts, and conclusions that make him "right in his own eyes!" The gift has attitude!

"Lord, please help him to see he has traded the truth for lies."

We are all stubborn on many things. The Scripture speaks a lot about the stubborn nature in all of us (Deuteronomy 9:13). However, why is it that some of our children yield their stubborn ways to God's love and some do not? Therein lies the problem! Who knows?

I do not know if Matthew will ever yield to God, but here are things I will continue to do as I follow the example of Moses in Deuteronomy chapter 9.

1. Faithfulness: we remind Matt how God has provided in huge ways.

2. Fall on my face before God and beg for mercy for Matt.

3. Fast and pray for godly sorrow to break through the pride.

4. Free Matthew to the God that created him.

5. Thank God for the gift of Matthew and our Melanie, who still hungers for God!

Prayer

Dear precious Lord, I thank You for our two beautiful children that You have given to Tim and me. They are true blessings. I pray and fast to call upon You to break through to Matthew's stubborn mindset that though he believes in You, he neither hungers for You, worships You, or seeks after Your will for his life. I pray that daily he would be reminded of all the times he experienced You and Your blessings in his youthful memories. I pray that You will visit him in dreams and call to him in conviction and love. Bring him to his senses, and help him have the courage to come back to You! Amen.

God Is Still in Control

Glenda Dillman
Maine District

"Let him have all your worries and cares, for he is always thinking
about you and watching everything that concerns you."
1 PETER 5:7 (TLB)

I started out thinking about this devotional in the middle of political
unrest as the 2020 elections neared, and it made me feel very nervous.
Now, we are in the depths of the worldwide COVID-19 pandemic. My
heart was very heavy with concern for our children and our grandchildren and what they may have to face in their lifetime.

God has been working on me through worship music, prayer, my devotions, scriptures, sermons, and more. God is reminding me over and over
that He is in control and that He loves our children and grandchildren
so much more than we do. God can handle anything, including what
we (or our children and grandchildren) face now or in the future. He
will raise up strong leaders that are grounded in the Word and will be
willing to stand up for what they believe, and they will speak the truth.

Here are some of the scriptures that have brought me from the worrying stage to the praising/thankful/restful stage:

"Rejoice in the Lord always. I will say it again: Rejoice! Let your
gentleness be evident to all. The Lord is near. Do not be anxious
about anything, but in every situation by prayer and petition with
thanksgiving, present your requests to God. And the peace of God,
which transcends all understanding, will guard your hearts and your
minds in Christ Jesus." Philippians 4:4-7

"Be strong and courageous. Do not be afraid; do not be discouraged, for the Lord your God will be with you wherever you go." Joshua 1:9

"Whoever dwells in the shelter of the Most High will rest in the shadow of the Almighty. I will say of the Lord, 'He is my refuge and my fortress, my God, in whom I trust.' Surely he will save you from the fowler's snare and from the deadly pestilence. He will cover you with his feathers, and under his wings you will find refuge; his faithfulness will be your shield and rampart. You will not fear the terror of night, nor the arrow that flies by day, nor the pestilence that stalks in the darkness, nor the plague that destroys at midday. A thousand may fall at your side, ten thousand at your right hand, but it will not come near you. You will only observe with your eyes and see the punishment of the wicked. If you say, 'The Lord is my refuge,' and you make the Most High your dwelling, no harm will overtake you, no disaster will come near your tent. For He will command His angels concerning you to guard you in all your ways; they will lift you up in their hands, so that you will not strike your foot against a stone. You will tread on the lion and the cobra; you will trample the great lion and the serpent. 'Because they love me,' says the Lord, 'I will rescue them; I will protect them, for they acknowledge my name. They will call on me, and I will answer them; I will be with them in trouble, I will deliver them and honor them. With long life, I will satisfy them and show them my salvation.'" Psalm 91:1-15

"Let Him have all your worries and cares, for He is always thinking about you and watching everything that concerns you." 1 Peter 5:7, TLB

"And now just as you trusted Christ to save you, trust Him, too, for each day's problems: live in vital union with Him." Colossians 2:6, TLB

In closing, instead of worrying, spend time in prayer and devotions for your children and grandchildren. Remember who God is and what He has done. Believe that God can handle whatever you, your children, and all future generations face.

Prayer

Lord Jesus, I praise You for how You love and care for each one of us. You have blessed us beyond measure, even in these most difficult times. Whatever we are going through now or in the future, You are our light in darkness, our guide, and promise keeper. We are surprised by things that happen, but nothing takes You by surprise. You are in control of everything, and You are faithful. Whatever we face or whatever we fear, You are with us. Help us keep our eyes fixed on You and not on the storm. Thank You that even though we do not know what the future holds, we can rest assured that You do. Amen.

Reliance on God: Parenting a Prodigal

Cindy Donley
Wisconsin District

"He says, 'Be still, and know that I am God; I will be exalted
among the nations, I will be exalted in the earth.'"
PSALM 46:10

"Trust in the Lord with all your heart and lean not on
your own understanding; in all your ways submit to
Him, and He will make your paths straight."
PROVERBS 3:5-6

God has given me these verses when I struggle with my prodigal's choices.

Parenting is challenging. I always thought that being the parent of adult children would be easy. I thought I would joyfully provide support and godly counsel as my children thrived, serving the Lord. For my "rule-following" children, those that embraced the values and methodologies we taught, including a close relationship with God, I have found that to be true. As for my prodigal, it's been painful to watch as she embraced worldly values and relationships that seemed unwise.

By nature, I am a "fixer." When I identify something broken, I want to fix it—immediately. When my prodigal was a child who would place herself in risky situations, I was able to protect her. I had control over her environment and could alter it to prevent her from being hurt. Now, as an adult, I have no control over her decisions or environment.

A couple of years ago, my daughter walked away from God and the church. She surrounded herself with dysfunctional individuals and embraced unhealthy relationships. She rejected our support and distanced herself from us.

After grappling with frustration and pain over her choices, I completely surrendered her to the Lord and trusted that He could "fix it" much better than I could. Whenever I was tempted to interfere, I tried to rely on past experiences where God had done the impossible, without my assistance. I would like to share one with you.

My mother was strong-willed and difficult to influence. She became angry with God after experiencing a divorce and her son's death. When I became a Christian as a teen, she wasn't happy. I witnessed to her and tried to be a Christian influence without any visible progress.

When I married my husband and followed him into ministry, I no longer had daily contact with her. Satan told me that I had sacrificed my mother's soul to help others find Christ. I continued to pray for her, but I didn't really think she would ever choose to be saved.

Decades later, my mother accepted Christ on her death bed. At her funeral, I was amazed to meet a parade of Christians who had regularly witnessed to her. All those years, I had no idea that anyone was witnessing to my mother. God had not abandoned her, even when she resisted. He answered my prayers by sending a strong Christian presence into her life.

I choose to believe that God will do the same for our prodigals. As for my daughter, God works in mysterious ways. A year ago, she remarried. She regularly attended her husband's church and returned to her relationship with the Lord. Unfortunately, her marriage is ending. My daughter is devastated, but she is relying on God, her church, and her family for support and comfort as she tries to put her life back together. While this is not the way I would have "fixed it," it is God's way, and I praise Him for it.

My daughter's story is not done, nor is God's work in your prodigal child's life. Trust and believe in Him; He will do whatever needs to be done for your child's salvation.

Prayer

Dear Lord, please surround our prodigals with Your influence and presence. Bring to their minds the many Christian lessons taught to them during their childhoods. Soften their hearts and give them a desire for a relationship with You. Bless the parents of our prodigals with the strength, patience, and self-control needed to allow You to work in Your way and Your timing in our children's lives. We give You the praise. Amen.

Trusting Him Who Builds the House

Maria Amelia Duarte
General Superintendent Spouse

"Unless the Lord builds the house, the builders labor in vain."
PSALM 127:1

In kindergarten, my notion of prayer was what the priest did in the rural Catholic church on special occasions. It sounded like mysterious talk until I learned that humans can have a conversation with God.

From grades one to six, my parents sent me to a school in the main town. Due to lack of transportation, I stayed with my uncle's family who lived very close to that school. I enjoyed the weekends with my parents and siblings but could not wait for Monday to hear my uncle's daily devotional for the family. In his prayers, he sounded as if he was having a normal conversation with one of us around the table. At times, my cousins and I wondered if we needed to learn my uncle's beautiful, musical way of talking with God to pray a "real prayer."

I tried to pray by myself, but none of them felt real until I was 13. It happened at an open-air service in front of my parents' home when the Nazarene preacher invited those who wanted to give their hearts to Jesus to show their hands. My mom and I prayed a sinner's prayer, and it was amazing to me that I also could have a conversation with God.

In my second prayer, I asked if He would give me a husband who could help me stay very close to Him in a devoted Christian family. My need to grow closer to God, as well as His answer to that prayer, made it clear to me that God wanted me doing my part in order for me to have the kind of family I desired.

As Psalm 127 says, "Unless the Lord builds the house, the builders labor in vain." Nobody should waste time and resources building their family on their own. All they need to do is to follow His lead in building up the family. Without prayer, I would never be able to take my role of spouse and parent because there is no spiritual health apart from God.

God has shown me that every day, several times, I need to pray for:

Wisdom — As parents, my husband and I need to model wisdom to our children by showing them that no decision is too small to be taken to God in prayer. We can get so used to doing certain things that we can easily think that we have become skilled enough to handle them without help.

Grace — The grace of God never stops working. I realize that I am a steward of His grace, not as someone responsible for making sure it is working but as a person responsible for sharing it with others. My husband and children are the first ones with whom I need to share grace.

Edification — Sometimes I am inclined to teach the good things I have learned from others in the same ways that I was taught. I need God to help me see new ways of teaching my family members that are effective and meaningful to their ways of thinking. God is never outdated.

Forgiveness — Ephesians 4:32 says "Be kind to one another, tenderhearted, forgiving one another, as God in Christ forgave you" (ESV). The ones who are closest to me can unintentionally do things that hurt me. Forgiving them makes me feel healthier, both spiritually and physically, and most of the times it does the same to the ones who need my forgiveness. It does even more if they ask forgiveness, but they do not have to. Being kind and tenderhearted is a great way of keeping our relationships healthy and pleasing to God.

Love — I am not able to fully describe the love of God, but each day I learn something new about it. His love cannot be contained. It overflows everywhere. I cannot think of any better setting where love can be enjoyed and shared than in the family, and I need to constantly be aware of my role in showing my family the many ways He loves us and enables us to love one another.

I like to interact with Joshua 24:14-15 where I hear God saying, "Now therefore fear the Lord and serve him in sincerity and in faithfulness" (v. 14, ESV) and by His grace I can respond, "as for me and my house, we will serve the Lord" (v. 15, ESV).

Prayer

Dear Lord, forgive us for the times when we have tried to do it on our own. It is an impossible task. We need You. Build our families, and they will please and serve You. Amen.

Broken Things

Jan Dunlop
Upstate New York District

"Let us hold unswervingly to the hope we
profess, for he who promised is faithful."
HEBREWS 10:23

As I think about the paths God has carried us along, I am reminded of all the times I did the same thing with my children. Toys on the floor, dirty faces, and temper tantrums are just a few things I remember about those days. No one ever told me how much easier raising toddlers is compared to watching our adult children make decisions!

Parents often find that adult children do not ask for or accept advice, yet when things get really tough, our children want to hear our voices.

I have often talked with moms whose hearts were breaking for their children. These children were raised right alongside mine, yet they chose paths that took them away from the Lord. I am reminded constantly that God allows us and our children to choose. Our labor in raising our children was not in vain, regardless of their choices, and our labor never ends, even if they make good choices.

Deuteronomy 7:6 says, "For you are a people holy to the Lord your God. The Lord your God has chosen you out of all the peoples on the face of the earth to be his people, his treasured possession."

I am chosen. You are chosen. Our kids are chosen. We are all chosen. God has chosen your prodigal, God is pursuing your prodigal, and God will put the right person in your prodigal's path at just the right time.

I found myself in the path of a prodigal at a district youth retreat. As I introduced myself to a young man sitting behind me, I realized that I had been praying for him for two and a half years already. His mother had asked me during our first summer on the district to pray for her son who was in prison. At the end of that morning's service at the young adult retreat, I turned around to talk with him again. When I looked closely at him, I asked, "Are you okay?" His reply was "No, I'm tired of living this life for myself and I need God to take over." Wow, what an answer! Those in the room gathered around him and began to pray.

This young man had searched in all the wrong places for happiness. His need for escape led him to bars and street corners for temporary, synthetic happiness in the form of alcohol and drugs. Time after time, overdose after overdose, he wondered why he lived when friends around him died. Eventually, he found himself addicted to heroin and in prison on felony drug charges.

Today he firmly believes he was saved by the grace of God thanks to the ceaseless prayers of his mother. He is now on a new path, sober and pursuing God's call in Bible college.

Our treasured possessions, our richest rewards can be won to the Lord! No one knows when or where they will come, but we can pray for God to put someone in their path. They won't think they deserve it anymore. They will think that they have messed up one too many times. The Holy Spirit will speak to them in a voice just right for the time when they are ready to surrender.

God is faithful and will answer our prayers at the right time. I believe this! The Holy Spirit can go anywhere, do anything, say anything, use anyone to bring them home!

The Holy Spirit uses broken things. But how does God use our broken heart, caused by our prodigals? He can use it to encourage others (especially after we surrender our prodigal to our Lord). He can use it to relate to a mom going through this pain for the first time. He can use our brokenness to see God's promise fulfilled. He can use the Holy Spirit to speak peace in the midst of our brokenness.

Prayer

Thank You, God, that no matter who we are, where we are, or who we are with, You can reach out and use us for Your glory. Please be with our treasured possessions, our richest rewards, that they will come to humble themselves before You. Bring them to the end of themselves. We pray that You take them through whatever it takes for them to draw close to You. We know You are pursuing them, so You are with them. Help them, Lord, to see You in a new way, a different way, a way that would drop them to their knees in search of You. You are an awesome God with awesome power, yet not controlling. Let Your Holy Spirit come and fill us with the hope that comes from You. Amen.

The Treasures of the Heart

Deb Eddings
Pittsburgh District

"But Mary treasured up all these things
and pondered them in her heart."
LUKE 2:19

I was in ninth grade when I felt a specific call to be a pastor's wife.

My oldest son, David, was five years old when God clearly revealed to me that I was raising a leader.

My middle son, Isaac, was eight years old when I had the privilege of kneeling next to him at an altar at children's camp where he allowed Jesus to come into his heart.

Tim, my youngest, was a senior in high school playing the cajón during our worship set when the Holy Spirit showed me that He was leading Tim in the rise and falls of beautiful worship music.

It is an incredible thing to know that God speaks to you and reveals truth that you can hold onto. And I have treasured up some of those things in my heart. I have been doing a lot of pondering of these treasures now that these kids of mine are navigating their young adult years.

Looking at the Word, Mary had some good things to treasure and ponder.

Gabriel, an archangel of God Almighty, came and visited her to deliver a life-changing message (Luke 1:30-33).

Shepherds came and shared an extraterrestrial encounter that happened to them because of the baby she was holding in her arms (Luke 2:16-18).

Simeon and Anna shared prophetic truths with her in the temple when she came to commit her newborn son to the God who fathered him (Luke 2:21-38).

She had much to treasure and ponder. And it would only increase as she and Jesus grew older. But these verses all revealed promises that she held onto. Promises that maybe as Jesus grew up, she said, "Really? Are you sure I heard that right so long ago? Maybe it was just a dream, not really God speaking to me."

I have asked those same questions, but God keeps His promises! Just because we can't see it or even believe it doesn't mean God hasn't promised it.

I went to Eastern Nazarene College to study Christian education knowing that God was preparing me for fulltime ministry other than the pastorate. When I met the male religion majors, I thought for sure I had misunderstood my calling from 9th grade. There was no way I was marrying any of those potential pastors!

David had some rough years that held some pretty bad choices during high school and early college. He was a leader for sure, but what is it that he would be leading?

Isaac, through the course of adolescence, developed quite a disdain for all things Christian.

Tim doesn't even play his cajón anymore.

Mary had no idea how the LORD would do what He promised. Everything about it seemed impossible as she saw her Son hanging on a cross. Does this mean that those things that God had promised meant nothing?

WE CAN TRUST THE PROMISES OF GOD.

I heard Dr. Stephen Manley say in a message once, "God operates out of the knowledge of all things." This has so shaped my thinking as I ponder these things treasured up in my heart. God didn't tell me all those things without knowing the choices my kids would make. He told me knowing everything about them. So, I treasure those things and ponder them in my heart, trusting the One who put them there.

Mary was last mentioned in Acts 1:13-14 after the ascension of Jesus. Would she ever know in her lifetime the entirety of the promise fulfilled? No. Will I ever know in my lifetime the fulfillment of the promises that God has given me about my children? Unknown. But what I do know is that these promises that God has given bring a hope that I can hold on to and treasure deep down in my heart.

I did marry a pastor.

David has had many leadership roles and continues to positively work out the details of the ministry call on his life.

Isaac has endured many hardships that keep him distant from the God who met him at an altar on that campground.

Tim is growing up and continues to be involved in things that can grow his faith. As far as the cajón, it is at least back in his possession!

Prayer

Papa, we come to You knowing that You operate out of the knowledge of all things. We cannot begin to know what is best for our children, but You know what's best and have their best interests in mind. Help us to trust You completely as we ponder what You promise. Amen and amen.

Take My Hand

Diane Estep
Kansas City District

"For I am the Lord your God who takes hold of your right
hand and says to you, Do not fear; I will help you."
ISAIAH 41:13

When our boys were little, I remember saying to them on many occasions, "Here, take my hand!" We would be crossing a busy street or walking through the grocery store. I needed to corral them, protect them, and keep them safe. And on occasion, I simply wanted to have them close!

Now that they are adults, I don't have quite that same ability. Can you picture me telling my 31-year-old son, "Josh, take your mother's hand as we walk through this intersection." Neither can I. However, it is so tempting at times to want to reach for their hand and guide them through hard situations or pull them by the hand out of tempting circumstances. But that's not my role now.

Years ago, an evangelist said in a sermon, "My hand of faith, in His Hand of power."

That, my friends, is our role as parents of adult children—keeping our hand of faith in the hand of the One who has the power to make a difference.

I've never forgotten that image and the importance of clinging to His hand. Isaiah 41:13 is a good reminder for me as a parent: "For I am the Lord your God who takes hold of your right hand and says to you, Do not fear; I will help you."

Can someone say, "Hallelujah!" He will help me. He will help you. He will help our children!

Earlier in chapter 41, Isaiah says, "I took you from the ends of the earth, from its farthest corners I called you. I said, 'You are my servant'; I have chosen you and have not rejected you. So, do not fear, for I am with you; do not be dismayed, for I am your God. I will strengthen you and help you; I will uphold you with my righteous right hand."

So, these thoughts are for you and me. Let's be reminded that:
We are His.
We don't need to fear.
He is with us.
He will strengthen and help us.
He will uphold us.
He will do the same for our children.

I don't know about you, but I'm clinging to His hand, even when my faith is as small as a mustard seed.

God cares for our kids even more than we do! His dreams and plans for them are bigger than we could ever dream. Take His hand. Trust His heart.

Prayer

Heavenly Father, we are clinging to Your hand today. We are trusting You to be with us as parents. Give us strength to weather tough days and give us wisdom on when to speak and when to be silent. We will hold Your hand and trust Your heart with our kids. Help us as parents to show Your grace to our kids. Place people in their lives that point them to You! Amen.

Light from Within

Pat Fitzpatrick
Canada Quebec District

"You are the light of the world. A town built on a hill cannot be hidden."
MATTHEW 5:14

I write this on our 43rd wedding anniversary. I met Ian in 1975 when I was a brand-new Christian. My parents were pastoring the Lurgan Church of the Nazarene in Northern Ireland. Ian had been brought up in the Methodist church and had become a Christian in May of that year on what could have been the last day of his life on earth. He was to have a major surgery, and his surgeon just happened to be a Methodist missionary home on furlough from Africa. After the surgery, he told Ian that his lungs had collapsed and there was nothing else they could do for him. He asked the doctors and nurses to bow their heads while he said a prayer for Ian, who had given his heart to the Lord the night before through the words and guidance of his dad, Tommy.

During that same time, a young man who was the youth leader in our church had been shot by terrorists on his way to work. He had jumped in front of the man that they were aiming at. At his hospital bedside, the Lord spoke to my dad, who was his pastor, and told him that Gerald would not survive and that He would send two men to take his place in the church. Gerald did die, and less than one month later, Ian walked into our Nazarene church with his friend Karl, who had been saved the same week at revival meetings in our town. They had both been members of a popular Irish rock band singing around the country. Ian was the lead singer and Karl the lead guitarist. They had disbanded a few months earlier due to the sectarian strife in Northern Ireland. These were the two young men.

Mum always invited the youth down to the parsonage, which was on the same grounds as the church. They would join us for supper after the Sunday evening service, and Ian and Karl came bringing their guitars. At the end of the evening, Ian asked if I would go out with him. Because of the nature of his illness, his body had been ravaged. He had lost 80 pounds. His hair had fallen out and I knew he had an ostomy bag, which he still has to this day. At the age of 20, everything for me was about the superficial, and I did not know what to do. Mum said just go for one date because you don't want to hurt him, and he would know why if I didn't go. So I did!

I believed God performed a miracle within me. I fell totally in love. Ian had a light from within that revealed the true beauty inside, and I saw that light!

There is an old movie that I have watched many times called *The Enchanted Cottage* in which only inside the cottage the plain girl looks beautiful to the man, and the man, whose face was badly disfigured in the war, looks normal to her. I believe that while we are in "the cottage" of God's light and love, we see things in people that others might not, and as long as we stay there, we will continue to see it.

In a world that seems to emphasize external beauty and builds multi-million-dollar industries around this false premise, I pray that we never forget that there is always much more to us than can be seen. May we be a people of inward beauty with the love of Jesus shining through us so that those around us can see it and feel it and aspire to have it for themselves.

Prayer

Dear Lord Jesus, give us the ability to see beyond what we can see with our eyes, to look upon everyone the way that You would look upon them, and to live our lives recognizing ALWAYS that while many look at the external, You look at the heart. In Jesus' name, amen.

In Prayer for My Husband

Candy Flores
South Carolina District

"I urge you, first of all, to pray for all people. Ask God to help
them; intercede on their behalf, and give thanks for them."
1 TIMOTHY 2:1 (NLT)

I feel that I am called to pray for my husband, and I found this calling
to be one of the greatest blessings in my life. Praying for my husband
throughout our ministry journey has been the best thing I can do for us.

Here are three things that I pray for my husband:

- I pray that his relationship with the Lord will grow stronger and
more intimate.

"Have I not commanded you? Be strong and courageous. Do not
be afraid; do not be discouraged, for the Lord your God will be
with you wherever you go." Joshua 1:9

- I pray that he would be a man of wisdom, compassion, understanding, and love to all.

"And this is my prayer; that your love may abound more and more
in knowledge and depth of insight, so that you may be able to dis-
cern what is best and may be pure and blameless for the day of
Christ." Philippians 1:9-10

- I pray that the Lord will use him as a servant and bless his work in all that he does for the Kingdom.

"For I know the plans I have for you, declares the Lord, plans to prosper you and not to harm you, plans to give you hope and a future." Jeremiah 29:11

Prayer

Father God, I thank You for this awesome and beautiful day You have blessed me and my family with. Once again, I have the privilege of praying a blessing over my husband and the leaders of the church. Lord, I pray for protection over all and God's direction in the work of His kingdom. Also, that our light may shine bright amongst all so they may see and feel Your presence. I pray that our conversation, attitude, and spirit may be Christlike. Thank You, LORD, for loving me and my family. I am honored to be a child of God and to serve alongside my husband in our calling to reach the lost. Amen.

In God's Waiting Room

Marsha Fountain
Louisiana District

"I wait for the Lord, my soul waits, and in his word
I hope; my soul waits for the Lord more than watchmen for
the morning, more than watchmen for the morning."
PSALM 130:5-6 (ESV)

Yes, I am in God's waiting room and it is not *Florida.

There is no musical interlude in God's waiting room. There are no outdated magazines. There are no amicable distractions to make the wait time pleasant. But, there is the presence of God and that is all that is needed.

The wait is longer than I anticipated. I am here waiting, praying, petitioning, interceding, praying, panting, pleading, whining, whimpering. Then I confess for the whining and whimpering and fortify myself with the Word.

Questions arise within me. Most days, I give God my questions. I am ashamed to admit that even now, on a few days I am guilty of picking up the questions, turning them, twisting them to look at each facet of the question. "Why do I have prodigal children?"

I have to surrender it to God. I have to surrender the self-protecting defenses such as remembering that Chuck and I have always prayed for our children; in utero to this very moment, we have prayed with our children and had devotions together. We had a family altar where we prayed together. We have such sweet memories of hearing their prayers.

Dwelling on this question is the very thing that could hinder my prayers for their salvation. I fall on my face before God and pray, "Here I am and here is my need. Oh, Dear God, here is my heart. Here is my troubled heart." I yield it all to God. My God. The God who gives me grace and strength. I surrender to the God who knows my name, the God who knows the names of my children and loves them, the God who longs for my prodigals to return to Him. Then, I am at rest (Philippians 4:6; Psalm 130:5-6; Micah 7:7). The additional benefit to this surrender is that I am better equipped to pray for my children.

As you have guessed, I am growing spiritually while in God's waiting room. Maybe this too will assist my prayers for my prodigals to return to the Lord. I am ever hopeful. My hope is well placed in my Lord and Savior.

Did I mention that I am in God's waiting room? Did I tell you that I have been here longer than expected? Way longer than I expected. I am not alone. God is with me. His Word encourages me as I continue to intercede for my precious children.

God hears my prayers. His Word is true, and He is worthy of my trust.

I pray for the precious names on our prayer list. According to God's Word, He never slumbers nor sleeps (Psalm 121:4). He is always on duty. Always. He is listening to our heart's cry for our children. He is faithful, so we can expect glorious answers from our great and mighty God (Galatians 6:3; Romans 15:13)!

*For non-Southerners, Florida is referred to in a humorous way as God's waiting room due to the high population of senior citizens.

Prayer

Father God, You are a loving God and You hear our prayers. I lift to You my children, my sisters, and their children. Hear our heart's cry. We wait expectantly before You, for You are our God. You are faithful. You are the God who hears and answers prayer.

A Hope for the Future

Kayla Gardner
Eastern Michigan District

> "This is what the Lord says: 'Restrain your voice from weeping
> and your eyes from tears, for your work will be rewarded,'
> declares the Lord. 'They will return from the land of the
> enemy. So there is hope for your descendants,' declares the
> Lord. 'Your children will return to their own land.'"
> **JEREMIAH 31:16-17**

We were greatly blessed to have two children birthed into our family, a girl and a boy. What a privilege and what a responsibility! We took parenting and developing their spiritual life seriously.

Our nightly routine went something like this: bathe, brush teeth, put on pajamas, then meet in the family room for prayers. After prayers, the children would go to their rooms and slip under the covers and wait for me to sit beside them and tell their personalized bedtime story. Each child heard a different story. They were the hero or the heroine. The name of the triumphant main character deviated only slightly from theirs. The story usually ended something like this: "and he (or she) was chosen for this wonderful reward because of his (or her) pure heart and great wisdom." The hope was they would always believe that a pure heart and wisdom from the Lord would be all they would need to accomplish great things for the Kingdom.

My husband and I prayed fervent prayers for each of our children, that they would be protected from temptation and would lead a life that would bring glory to God. But they each had their struggles and chose to walk paths we had not anticipated. Our daughter listened to God's call on her life and chose to launch out with unbridled courage into missions in a creative access country. Our son chose to express his God-given talents in ways that do not glorify Him and broke our hearts.

It has been a long and weary journey through teenage, college, and now adult years. Many days, the sorrows of witnessing our son behave in self-destructive and disrespectful ways have been oppressive.

Finally, I realized that my attitude was not glorifying the Lord. I began to dig into Scripture, read every Christian book on the subject of the "prodigal child," and talk to other parents about how they were coping. I heard a lot and learned much.

I have come to three conclusions that bring me hope and most days joy.

1. God loves my child more than I do.

2. He cares more about my child's salvation than I can comprehend.

3. He is much more capable of convicting my child than I am.

My anxious hand-wringing and tears were doing nothing for my relationship with my son. Neither was it glorifying God. We now pray daily for our son, thanking the Lord for His love for him and how He is at work to reach our son. I also love to collect stories of how people have turned to the Lord in their adult years. I continue to read books on prodigals, dive into Scripture, and talk to other hurting parents, but my attitude and perspective are different now. I am thankful that the Lord is working in ways I cannot see, loves me more than I can comprehend, and knows exactly how to reach my prodigal child. My confidence is found in Jeremiah 31:16-17.

Prayer

O precious Jesus, thank You so very much that we can bring our children, our richest rewards, to You! Thank You that You love them more than we do and more than we can possibly comprehend.

Thank You, Lord, that You are actively pursuing their hearts of stone to soften them and turn them to You. You were crucified and resurrected to save them from the destruction of sin.

Thank You, Lord, that we can trust You because You are infinitely more capable of convicting our children through the Holy Spirit than we are with our simple words. We rejoice in the hope that one day our family will all be of one mind and spirit as we call You Heavenly Father and Lord. Amen.

Sit Yourself Down!

Leslie Garman
Los Angeles District

"Jesus was placed before the governor, who questioned Him:
'Are you the 'King of the Jews'?' Jesus said, 'If you say so.' But
when the accusations rained down hot and heavy from the
high priests and religious leaders, He said nothing. Pilate asked
Him, 'Do You hear that long list of accusations? Aren't You
going to say something?' Jesus kept silence—not a word from
His mouth. The governor was impressed, really impressed."
MATTHEW 27:11-14 (MSG)

This one-sided dialogue took place in the courtyard of the palace. As
Jesus was brought to the enclosure, Pilate arrived. As Pilate was governor, his staff surely wasted no time in providing a temporary throne: the
curule seat. Taken from the word "chariot," a curule seat was a symbol
of political or military position. The uncomfortable seat ensured that
the official would carry out his duty in a timely and efficient manner. By
sitting on this foundation, Pilate transformed any area into a courtroom.

Today, in 2020, as I write this, we are in the midst of the COVID-19
pandemic, and life—including church and fellowship—has been completely upended. (My husband, Greg, just returned from Peru, where
he stayed for an additional 10 days as the borders closed down—I am
glad to have him home!)

I would like to invite you to join me in sitting not at the curule seat but
at the mercy seat. The mercy seat was a gold lid placed on the Ark of the
Covenant. This lid created a space in which Yahweh was to appear. For
us today, we could say that this space provides access and communion.

If Pilate could render any territory judicial by the sitting in the chair, could we possibly render any territory grace-filled and Jesus-like by seating ourselves—daily and in any capacity—in God's mercy seat? I believe so.

Friends, sit yourself down. Are you surrounded by isolation? Is disease threatening your hope? Are you kept awake because of worry over your children? How about the balance in your checking account? Perhaps the giving of your tithe has taken on a completely new challenge. Do you cover your head from the hurts of the past?

The song "Mercy Seat" describes someone running to the mercy seat, not crawling, sauntering, or strolling. I challenge all of us—you and me—to run to the mercy seat today. I am going to "one-up" the challenge: Tell someone that you are placing yourself there! I have found that as the spouse of a district superintendent, I have to be much more intentional about finding my bearings as a witness for Jesus Christ. It is much easier to invite someone to sit with me in church. I don't think that the one I'm witnessing to would be very interested in traveling around with me on most Sundays!

Pilate saw something different in Jesus Christ: No panic. No excuses. No anger. No fear. Just different.

Friends, may we emulate our Messiah just as He emulated His Father: with mercy, with grace, with conversation when it's "Godly-timed." May we be different, and sit ourselves down on the mercy seat.

Prayer

God, thank You for Your Son. Thank You that in these strange times, nothing is strange to You. Thank You for Your creativity and the technology needed during this season. Lord, may we sit ourselves down at Your mercy seat today and invite someone to sit with us. Bless our spouses—may we be a joy to them. Bless our churches, and may we look back, at some point, and say "This was the greatest day—so far—for our churches!" In Your precious, patient, gentle, majestic name we pray, amen.

Praying God's Promises

Jackie Gilmore
Northern Michigan District

"I will instruct you and teach you in the way you should
go; I will counsel you with my loving eye upon you."
PSALM 32:8

I became a first-time grandma this year! Elena Mercedes Ricápito arrived February 16, 2020, and she has stolen my heart in a way that I had never imagined possible. As I held this precious little girl in my arms, I was flooded with memories of being a new mother. The love that overwhelmed me so many years ago as I held my own children for the first time was making its way back into my heart, and I realized the great blessing and responsibility of having another precious child to lift in prayer.

Many years ago, I selected Psalm 32:8 as my life verse. In claiming that promise for my own life, I have also claimed it for my children and now my grandchild. God's Word is full of promises for us to cling to and affirm. I think God wants us to search His word and claim His promises for our lives. I have been praying for my children since the day I learned of their creation, and I have trusted God to do a work in each of their lives. God's promise of instruction and guidance seems to always be interwoven throughout my prayers for them. As they have grown and matured, there have obviously been different and specific needs that I have lifted in prayer for each of them. Though not sure how God would choose to answer each one, I trusted that He would work and answer in the best way for each need for their good and for His glory.

As Christians, we are all praying for the salvation of the children He has placed in our lives. These may be our own children and grandchildren or the children of someone else that we love. Although each child must make his or her own choice, we can be assured that God always desires to answer this prayer with a resounding YES! "The Lord is not slow about His promise, as some count slowness, but is patient toward you, not wishing for any to perish but for all to come to repentance" (2 Peter 3:9). God loves our children more than we do! So dear ones, as we continue to lift our loved ones to the Father who loves them most, I want to encourage you, and remind myself, to persevere in prayer and to wait patiently to see the good that God will do in their lives and to claim the promises He gives us that He will do it!

Prayer

Heavenly Father, thank You for Your wonderful blessings in our lives. Our family members, our children, and our grandchildren are our most precious treasures. Our heart's desire is that they will come to know You as their personal Savior, to know the joy of living a life complete in You. Help us to spiritually nurture and pray for them. May we boldly claim the precious promises that You have given to us in Your Word. We pray in Jesus' name, amen.

When Life Doesn't Go as Planned

Sharon Graves
General Superintendent Spouse

"Then you will call on me and come and pray to me, and
I will listen to you. You will seek me and find me when you
seek me with all your heart. I will be found by you," declares
the Lord, "and will bring you back from captivity."
JEREMIAH 29:12-14a

We all experience times in our lives when things do not go as we planned. Our family went through a difficult situation that lasted years. I admit I did not handle it well. At first, it was easy to pray and trust, believing God would give us the answer we desired. However, as time went on with no answers, the situation became my obsession. I focused on fixing, not on God. Trust became a major issue. Worry and fear controlled my life and clouded my view of God. My heart was breaking as I helplessly watched my son struggle. Pain was everywhere.

Looking back, I thought my faith and trust in God would have been strong enough to carry me through. The pain of unanswered prayer became a wall separating me from God. I knew He could do anything, but for some reason He was choosing not to fix this problem. Finally, in March 2010, I reached a breaking point. Alone for two days straight, I decided I needed to bare my soul to God and try to understand Him. I started by telling Him everything, including being hurt and disappointed that He hadn't worked this out.

The Lord was close to me that night and the following days. His presence could be felt. He heard and came to me. I opened His Word and the underlined verses from previous times began to speak to me and bring me peace.

"'For I know the plans that I have for you,'" declares the Lord, "plans to prosper you and not to harm you, plans to give you a hope and a future.'" Jeremiah 29:11

"Arise, cry out in the night, as the watches of the night begin; pour out your heart like water in the presence of the Lord. Lift up your hands to him for the lives of your children." Lamentations 2:19

"Because of the Lord's great love we are not consumed, for his compassions never fail. They are new every morning; great is your faithfulness." Lamentations 3:22-23

All through the Psalms, we are told to rest in Him, to rejoice in the Lord continually, to sing to Him, and to trust in Him.

It is hard to trust when you feel hurt so deeply, when you don't understand. I was staring at the problem and only glancing at God. He was to be my attention. The more I looked to Him, the more peace came into my heart and mind.

"Then you will call upon me and I will listen ... seek me with all your heart ... I will be found by you and will bring you back." Jeremiah 29:12-14

That was what I needed to hear, what I needed to do. Waiting for answers can be frustrating and can distract you from remembering all you know, in your mind and heart, about God. How did I let worry consume me? How did I ever doubt my Lord? God is the same yesterday, today, and forever. He is a God of love, more than I will ever be able to comprehend. He never left me.

Once I released control to Him, God answered in ways we never imagined. He turned our pain into joy and chaos into order. He restored me back into fellowship before the miracles happened. Then, firsthand, I saw God work a miracle—actually three miracles in this situation!

Today, in the situations I face, I trust more. The lessons I learned from this journey have equipped me to be stronger. I cannot promise you God is going to answer your prayers in the way you want or desire, but

I know firsthand that God can be trusted. I have experienced His love, His presence, and healing in the lowest places of my life.

Our children and grandchildren are blessings we treasure. As strong as our love is for them, God loves them more. Prayer is not a single action but a lifestyle we live, so we lift them to God in prayer, believing He will work in their lives.

Prayer

Thank You, Lord, for who You are. Thank You for Your love that is unconditional, overwhelming, and beyond comprehension. In times when we doubt, even turn away, we thank You for Your patient and welcoming love. We know that with You, the pain and distress that come into our lives are a part of the beautiful tapestry You are creating. May we continue to pray for our family and trust the results to You. Amen.

Watching and Waiting

Karan Gunter
MidSouth District

> "But as for me, I watch in hope for the Lord,
> I wait for God my Savior; my God will hear me."
> MICAH 7:7

Watching… waiting… watching… and waiting some more! These days have had all of us watching and waiting, haven't they? Watching the news, waiting for directives, watching our screens, waiting for test results, watching our distance, waiting for reopening.

As a little girl, I remember waiting for my dad to come home from work. He was career Army, and when we lived on post, that meant at 5 o'clock we would hear the melody of "Retreat." This signaled the regular duty day, a long, hard day of work, was over—it was an ending.

For us, however, it was a beginning. Daddy was headed home! My ears would perk up as I heard the bugles; I would head for the window and I would watch. I didn't just look out the window occasionally; I'd stand at the window and peer down the street. I knew he was coming, so I would stay there until he came. I was watching for his car, for him. I never had my mind on what he would do once he got home. I was just waiting for him to be home. I was watching for someone, not something.

In much the same way, once my kids were driving, I watched for them! On nights they were later than expected, as the long minutes passed, my body would tense, my breathing would quicken, my patience would thin…but when headlights would beam into the window as they turned into the driveway, my shoulders relaxed, my breathing slowed, and my soul would rest. They were home.

The past few years have found me at the window... watching and waiting on behalf of one of our children. I have been waiting for a long, difficult season to end—watching to see what the Lord is going to do, how He will redeem, and when He will create a new beginning.

But as for me, I watch in hope for the Lord, I wait for God my Savior; my God will hear me.

Several times, Micah 7:7 has come up in my readings. Each time, my ears have perked up, and in a sense, I have run to the window, watching and waiting for something to happen—with a little fear and trepidation—but watching and waiting all the same. Most recently, however, when the verse appeared again, as my ears perked in recognition, my heart fluttered and began to hope. The Holy Spirit began to remind me. It is not about watching and waiting for the what and the how and the when—it's all about the Who!

HE has come! The tiny baby in Bethlehem, the redeeming Rabbi at Zacchaeus' house, the suffering Servant on the cross, the risen Savior on the way to Emmaus, and the wind of His Spirit in Jerusalem... in each stage, His coming brought a new beginning!

As I continue to pray and affirm this scripture around my children and grandchildren each day, I'm reminded that my God has heard me, He will continue to hear me, and He will hear you, too, as you watch and wait for Him. It is just the beginning.

Prayer

Our very present God, sometimes situations in life and with our children have us standing at the window. The circumstances may sound like bugles tempting us to retreat. They may create doubt, fear, and anxiety and even feel like an ending. But help us to keep watching and waiting for You with a hopeful heart. We entrust our children—and their new beginnings—to You. Amen.

Believing, Trusting, Pressing On

Patti Hartley
Alaska District

"He alone is my refuge, my place of safety;
he is my God, and I trust Him."
PSALM 91:2 (NLT)

In looking through my journal over the last few years of struggle with having prodigal children, I see tears, doubt, fear, blame, and discouragement. But I also see that those moments are filled with a continual surrender and trust in Jesus—a continual surrender to the One who understands, loves, and cares for me and my children more than I ever could imagine possible.

When our daughter came to us a few years ago and told us she was expecting a baby out of wedlock, my world seemed to cave in. The guilt and the blaming started, not against my daughter but against me. Questions started flooding my mind. Where did I go wrong? Where have I failed? What could I have done differently? Being raised in an alcoholic and drug abused family, I had the misconception that if I loved Jesus and married someone who loved Jesus—especially someone who was going into ministry—then life would be perfect (whatever "perfect" is supposed to be in today's world)! We would serve Jesus as a family by having family devotions, prayer, and worship as we attend church together, which we did faithfully. My thoughts were that if I loved Jesus and served Him with my whole heart, then my kids would automatically love and serve Jesus with all of their hearts and days.

Oh, how I wish I could take away their free will! But God gives us the choice to serve Him or not. Even now, my heartaches and longs for the day when I see them loving and walking with Jesus.

The bright spot is that our lives have been so blessed by a little boy that God brought into our lives through circumstances that have stretched us, molded us, and helped us love unconditionally (only by God's grace, mercy, and love).

I am reminded of the following scriptures.

"The struggle is not with (child's name) but with the spiritual forces that influence them to turn away from you." Ephesians 6:12

"Give all your worries and cares to God for He cares for you." 1 Peter 5:7

"He alone is my refuge, my place of safety; he is my God and I trust Him." Psalm 91:2

"All things are possible with God." Mark 10:27

Jesus knows every prayer spoken, and He hears the cries of our hearts. There is no greater sense of joy and peace than seeing throughout Scripture that God deeply cares about what we are going through. Hope and peace can be ours when we believe that in God's timing and in His ways, He will answer our hearts cries. Jesus is never blind to our tears, never deaf to our prayers, and never silent to our pains. He sees, He hears, and He will deliver. I so long to see the fruit of our prayers, love, fasting, and surrendering in the form of our children giving their all to Jesus. But for now, let's keep trusting, keep pressing on, and keep believing because God is faithful, and someday our children will love, walk, and serve Jesus, for it is God's will that they come to know and believe in Him.

Prayer

My precious Jesus, thank You for Your faithfulness and help in our bad days and good days. Thank You for never leaving us nor forsaking us. Thank You for blessing our lives with our children. They are truly one of the greatest gifts and blessings we could ever receive from You. Thank You for loving our children more than we ever think possible. We know that it is Your desire that our children accept You as their Savior. We pray according to Your will that our children will accept You, love You, and walk with You. We pray that You would break every stronghold and chain of the enemy in their lives. Reveal Yourself to them and draw them to You so that they can't get away from Your presence and help. By faith, I will keep on trusting, keep on believing, and keep pressing on in my love for You, in my love for my children, and in my daily walk and prayers. It is in Jesus' name I pray according to Your will, amen.

God's Transgenerational Faithfulness

Aurora Herrera
Texas-Oklahoma Latin District

"Know therefore that the Lord your God is God; he is the faithful
God, keeping his covenant of love to a thousand generations
of those who love him and keep his commandments."
DEUTERONOMY 7:9

I enjoy the moments I spend at home with my two little granddaughters, especially in this season that we must be at home because of the COVID-19 pandemic. One of those favorite moments is before supper. Every day, Deia, my five-year old granddaughter, asks to pray for the meal. This is her daily prayer: "Thank you Jesus for my mommy, poppy, litos, cousins, my family, and for all the people in the world who are suffering because of the coronavirus." Her prayer blesses my heart not just because of her tender age but because she herself is the answer to much prayer. We call her our little miracle.

Our daughter Denia's dream when she got married was to have a baby. With sadness, we saw her lose her first baby. The following year she lost her second. The third year she lost her third baby, and in five years she had lost six babies. She was about to give up, but God had not forgotten her. Prayer, faith in God, and believing in His promises have all been a vital part of our family. We have tried to teach our children to have faith in God in spite of the circumstances. As she was going through her ordeal, we never stopped asking God for a miracle for our daughter. Our granddaughter was born nine months after much prayer and fasting. We praise God for His answer to our prayer! Our daughter finally was able to say like Hannah, "I prayed for this child, and the Lord has granted me what I asked of him. So now I give her to the Lord" (1 Samuel 1:27-28a).

Through the years, we have experienced God's grace on our family. He has been with us as we have raised three children, all of them married now and having their own families. Imprinted in my mind are those moments when they were small. We would kneel together to pray when they were going through difficult times (we still do the same now that they are adults). It blesses me to see how they do the same with their own children, creating faith in their little minds.

I come from a large family. I am a third-generation Nazarene. My grandparents were pioneer pastors with the Church of the Nazarene in Mexico. They were instrumental in developing my love for the Lord and my faith in Him. Etched in my mind, as well, is an image of them praying for me when I was a little girl. My constant prayer is that I may be able to do the same with my grandchildren, teaching them to love and to have faith in the Lord.

I am enjoying this beautiful season in my life, grandmother to six grandchildren, ages six, five, four, three, three, and one. They will face a very different world than mine; they will live in very difficult times. To inculcate love and faith in God in their little minds is of vital importance.

I feel that it is part of my responsibility to teach them that God is faithful and that He keeps His promises and loves those who love Him.

Prayer

Thank You, Lord, because You have been faithful through the generations. I pray for my grandchildren, that with Your help they may become the fifth generation of God-fearing Nazarenes. Seasons come and go, and so do generations, but Your steadfast love remains. Help them grow to become useful servants in Your kingdom, and may they teach their children to fear and love You so that Your faithfulness will continue through more generations. In Jesus' wonderful name, amen.

For Him

Jeanna Hoffman
Prairie Lakes District

"And the King will say, 'I tell you the truth, when you did it to one of
the least of these my brothers and sisters, you were doing it to me!'"
MATTHEW 25:40 (NLT)

My husband's birth father abandoned Steve and his mother when Steve
was nine months old. Then, when he was seven years old, Steve's mother
died of leukemia. His mother had several siblings and half siblings.
There was much discussion among them as to who would take Steve
in and raise him. They all had reasons not take him, whether because
of inconvenience or finances.

Steve's half-uncle Duane and wife, Laverne, said that they would take
him into their home. They were not wealthy and had a small home. Both
Duane and Laverne's extended family voiced concerns to them: "you
already have two children;" "you don't have room;" "you can't afford
to raise another child." Their response was, "we may not have many
things or a big house, but we have room in our heart for him."

Steve was taken in by Duane and Laverne and raised as one of their
own. They were a strong Christian family that taught him to love Jesus
and showed him the love of Christ in daily life. He will tell you that
they are truly his father and mother, and he would not be where he is
today if it weren't for them.

As we are going through our daily lives and are focused on our sched-
ules and our own families, do we see or hear those around us who may
need our attention, love, or a kind word? We can easily find excuses
why we are not the ones to meet that need—work, children, housework,

grandchildren, fatigue, and other distractions. I can find myself saying and thinking these things. May we not be the ones who say we don't have room in our lives but may we be the ones who say, "we have room in our hearts."

Prayer

Lord, open our eyes and our hearts to see others as You see them and to see their needs. By serving others, we are showing Your love to them and our love for You.

Prevailing Prayer Works Both Ways

Dinah Huff
Georgia District

"Oh, the depth of the riches of the wisdom and knowledge of God!
How unsearchable His judgments, and His paths beyond tracing out!"
ROMANS 11:33

God has the final word. He knows where we are and what concerns us at this moment. For every promise He has made He will never change. Even though it may appear that nothing is happening, God is at work—behind the scenes, in the background, accomplishing His purpose. Patience is needed to see God's promises fulfilled in His people.

Isaiah 55:8-9 says, "'For my thoughts are not your thoughts, neither are your ways my ways,' declares the Lord. 'As the heavens are higher than the earth, so are my ways higher than your ways and my thoughts than your thoughts.'" Close your eyes and think of a situation (son, daughter, etc.) that you are holding onto in prevailing prayer. Dr. Earl Lee, former missionary to India and pastor said, "If you are holding onto a situation longer than 24 hours, then you haven't committed it to God."

Psalm 37 is our security as we trust in Him. Do not FRET (Fear, Resentment, Envy, Tension).

Trust in the Lord and do good (Proverbs 3:5-6).

DELIGHT yourself in the Lord (Daily Everything Laid Into God's Hands Triumphantly).

Commit your way to the Lord (1 Timothy 1:18-19)

Rest in the Lord and wait patiently for Him (Philippians 2:13).

Thank Him (Peace comes with thanksgiving). When you commit something or someone or a situation into God's hands, then let go and thank Him that He is working His ultimate plan out in His perfect timing.

Walking with and abiding in Christ constantly reminds us that God is in control of all things. He is our peace, our hope, our joy. Celebrate knowing that Jesus Christ always makes a difference in every situation as we totally commit all things into His hands.

Prayer

Heavenly Father, I praise Your precious name. Thank You for Your loving kindness, mercy, grace, and peace. You are the well spring of my life, and I trust You completely. I cast all my cares upon You and I wait in expectation of how You will answer and provide. Amen!

The Greatest Farewell Gift

Christine Youn Hung
Northern California District

"Now to him who is able to do immeasurably more than all
we ask or imagine, according to his power that is at work
within us, to him be glory in the church and in Christ Jesus
throughout all generations, for ever and ever! Amen."
EPHESIANS 3:20-21

I will always remember the last sermon I gave to my beloved Trinity Church family. Sermon prep was agonizing to say the least. My heart was full of love, full of grieving, and full of expectation all at the same time. What could I possibly say that could communicate all I have felt for the people I have cared for these past 14 years? What final message was the centerpiece of all my hopes and dreams for them? After much meditation, reflection, and prayer, it all bubbled down to one simple sentence: Jesus loves me, this I know.

I wanted them to know, to really know, that Jesus loves them with a love that is incomprehensible, indescribable, transformational, unconditional; a love that rebuilds, restores, repairs, renews, and refreshes. Did our church have a deep knowledge of this kind of love?

In the original Greek, the word for "knowledge" is *gnósis*. This kind of knowledge doesn't come from hearing it second-hand. It doesn't come from reading a textbook. It comes from first-hand experience, gained only through a direct relationship. Deep within my pastoral heart, I wanted these dear people to know and experience the profound love of Jesus Christ. I wanted them to know that Jesus loves them with as much passion and intensity as the Father loves His Beloved Son.

At the end of the sermon, I gave an altar call. There were three individuals I had in mind. With my eyes closed, I listened to the worship team and prayed silently, fervently, for these three people: Lord, pretty, pretty please? What a gift it would be for these three people to receive Christ during my final sermon! What a reward for all my faithful prayers and dedicated service!

Now I realize just how self-absorbed I was being. I mean, really, what does the salvation of others have to do with me and my rewards? Nevertheless, I prayed with all my heart and felt certain that the air was thick with expectancy. My prayers were going to be answered!

When I opened my eyes, they instantly filled up with tears. I could feel my heart pounding in my chest, about ready to burst. Standing before me, with her hands clasped tightly together, her head bowed down, and tears flowing from her cheeks, was my 12-year-old daughter.

As a mother and as a pastor, I could not think of a more precious gift than that. How many nights have I spent praying over her? How many years have I watched her grow, anxious that I wasn't doing a good job? How many times have I fretted at how ministry might be affecting our children?

My prayers were indeed answered. I felt God's presence as I wrapped my arms around her and prayed a prayer of joyful celebration and gratitude. I sensed the Lord telling me that in my obedience to love faithfully in my ministry, and through the love and support of my church family, and, of course, the persistent beckoning from their Heavenly Father, my children were experiencing the love of Jesus for themselves. I looked around to see that there was not a dry eye in the sanctuary.

Our last day at Trinity Church, we celebrated seven baptisms. Two of our oldest children were among them. I don't know when the other two will follow. I don't know if or when pitfalls, distractions, or times of crisis will draw my children away. I do know that God answers prayers and as much as we, as parents, long for it, God passionately desires to see all our children to know Him and experience the love of Jesus first hand.

Prayer

I pray that from His glorious, unlimited resources, He will empower you with inner strength through His Spirit. Then Christ will make His home in your hearts as you trust in Him. Your roots will grow down into God's love and keep you strong. And may you have the power to understand, as all God's people should, how wide, how long, how high, and how deep His love is. May you experience the love of Christ, though it is too great to understand fully. Then you will be made complete with all the fullness of life and power that comes from God (Ephesians 3:16-21, NLT).

Praying God's Will as We Abide in Him

Mary Johnston
South Central Ohio District

"I am the vine; you are the branches. If you remain in me and
I in you, you will bear much fruit; apart from me you can
do nothing ... If you remain in me and my words remain in
you, ask whatever you wish, and it will be done for you."
JOHN 15:5, 7

How can it be that some prayers are answered with a "yes" and others are not? As I think about some of my prayers that have been answered with a "yes" and prayers that have been answered with a "no" or even silence on God's part, I recognize that some were prayed specifically with His guidance while others included asking God for "good" things. If I "remain" in Jesus, I will be careful to follow and accept His directions. Those answered prayers from the past encourage me.

When our sons were in grade school, we moved to Paris. We were finding it impossible to find an affordable house that would rent to missionaries. I sensed that our sons needed stability and a feeling of being "at home." I felt compelled by the Lord to ask our boys what they especially wanted in a home. One son wanted an apple tree (in a Paris suburb???), and our yard had an apple tree. My husband and I wanted a guest room so I didn't have to move the boys around every time we had guests (a common occurrence). Trevor wanted a wood burning fireplace, and we got that too. It was a wonderful place that felt like home from day one even though the purple bedroom carpet and a purple tiled bathroom were not to my taste.

This was not the only prayer answered for our sons. We prayed that the cruelty one son experienced in school would not permanently affect him; now he doesn't even remember it. After a year of school in the USA, going back into the French system was exceptionally challenging. A few weeks into school, one son said, "I might as well quit trying. It isn't doing any good." My desperate whispered prayer then was, "God, You will have to help him. I can't." The next exam, he was back on track and doing well.

God loves our children even more than we do. One prayer we can pray confidently—knowing it is in His will—is that they come to know Him and serve Him as Savior and Lord. I believe He can guide us to pray specifically for circumstances He can use to draw them to Himself.

Remembering those times when He stepped in and gave a "good gift," sometimes in seemingly unimportant ways (apple tree), helps me trust Him when His answer is not what I hoped for. In a tragic circumstance that God allowed to continue despite my prayers and fasting, I learned to submit my will to Him and ask Him to redeem the situation for His kingdom.

Trusting God with ourselves and our loved ones AND desiring God's will above all else are ways to submit to God. I have not always been successful in this and have sometimes been resigned, even resentful or doubtful, when God allowed tragedy and failed to provide miracles.

Let's remind ourselves of answered prayers and an unchanging God. Let's draw closer to Him wholeheartedly trusting in the One who sacrificed everything for us. After all, God loves us and our children more than we can imagine!

Prayer

Heavenly Father, thank You for Your love for each of us and for the privilege of prayer. Draw our children and their families close to You. May they accept Your wonderful gift of salvation and live in step with You. Guide us in our prayers that we might ever keep Your will as a priority. Keep us faithful in our prayers for all people and Your purposes, and help us to recognize Your answers and give You the praise and glory. Amen.

Lessons Learned by the Parents of a Prodigal

Anonymous

"But while he was still a long way off..."
LUKE 15:20b

I don't have a success story to share with you...yet. Though our prodigal has made great progress toward addiction recovery, she is still a long way off. Even though her journey back home is not complete, there are a few important lessons I've learned.

- I shouldn't let my child's failures become my identity. Though I was by no means the perfect parent, my daughter's failures are not my own.

- I shouldn't be so consumed by my prodigal's desperate condition that I neglect my relationship with my other children or my spouse.

- I shouldn't give in to despair or forsake my joy in the Lord. He hasn't forgotten our prodigal. In fact, even while she is still a long way off, He sees her and loves her with a Father's heart of compassion.

- Every situation is different. Each parent's experience with a prodigal child brings a unique brand of pain. Instead of saying you understand, offer a word of non-judgmental support such as, "I'm sorry you're going through this. I can't begin to imagine your pain."

I lost count, years ago, of the number of times a well-intentioned believer quoted the following scripture to me: "Train up a child in the way he should go…" I understand their desire to encourage a hurting parent by assuring that their prodigal will return. I can relate to the need to say something, anything, to fill the silence. I also understand that this verse is true—and yet, I also know that God has granted to each of us free will to accept the way of righteousness or to go our own rebellious way. He won't force anyone to follow Him, no matter how His heart must break at the rejection.

I must confess, whenever someone quotes the "Train up a child" verse to me, I find myself fighting the temptation to hear the subtext behind their words as "…this means you must not have done a very good job of training your child or they would have never departed from it." I sense, whether true or not, that my child-rearing skills are being called into question and compared alongside the speaker's seemingly expert parenting and model family. Whenever I'm tempted to entertain these thoughts, I shamefully look back on a day long ago when I took personal (sinful) credit for the fact that my children rarely embarrassed us, much less strayed from the straight and narrow.

However, in the 15 years since my prodigal's wanderings began, I have learned well the lessons of humility and true compassion and empathy for those who, through no fault of their own, must live through the shame and sorrow of a child's sinful choices. Never again will I entertain such pride.

The most helpful words of encouragement I've received from concerned friends have been some form of the following: "Whenever the Lord brings your daughter to mind, I pray for her and ask Him to send someone along her path that will minister to her and use them to bring her back to the fold." As I envision the Lord answering that prayer, I am able to rest in the knowledge that God is in charge. He loves her more than I ever could, although I cannot humanly understand how that is possible. He wants what is best for her. And He is wooing her back to Him, using those whose ears are tuned to hear the voice of God as He calls them to act.

Though my child is still a prodigal, I remain optimistic. While I don't have a success story to tell yet, my faith is unwavering. In fact, I am more convinced than ever that God is at work, wooing our prodigal back into the fold. He sees and loves our wayward child even though she is still "a long way off."

Prayer

Dear loving Heavenly Father, even when we were a long way off, You saw us. Your heart was filled with overwhelming, unconditional love. You welcomed us home.

Now, as we come to You, broken in spirit over our wayward children, we know You are eager to greet them with open arms when they, at last, run from their rebellious ways and return home where they belong. Today, Father God, will You send someone across our prodigal's path who You can use to remind them of Your love, Your mercy, Your grace... someone who will serve as a positive influence to draw them even one step closer to a journey of healing and restoration.

We commit our prodigal to You, knowing that You love them more than we ever could! Amen.

Raising Independent Children

Sharon Kester
Washington Pacific District

"Start children off on the way they should go, and even
when they are old they will not turn from it."
PROVERBS 22:6

Why is it that when you raise independent children, you are surprised when they become independent? My husband and I were in way over our heads with our strong-willed child. He didn't sleep. He controlled our lives and household. We sought help from our doctor, who was a godsend! One technique the doctor taught us was to use the word "negotiable." Everything was negotiable except moral or safety issues. We learned that we needed to give him choices so that he would have a sense of power and ownership.

One day after dinner, we wanted him to get his bath and get ready for bed. He didn't want to, but instead of a temper tantrum, he asked, "Is this negotiable?" We replied, "Yes, actually it is. Do you have a better suggestion?" He asked, "Can I get my bath after I watch a cartoon?" Great idea! End of discussion; everyone is happy. Was it always that simple? No, but it helped us understand how his mind worked, and we were training him up correctly for his personality—the way God created him—and no one was getting hurt. Ephesians 6:4, "Fathers, do not exasperate your children; instead bring them up in the training and instruction of the Lord."

We constantly told him that we were disciplining him now so that he could discipline himself later. The older he got, that is exactly what happened, and we couldn't have been prouder. We were so thankful that we put in those hard days, weeks, months, early on in his life.

After 15 years of youth ministry, we moved to accept our first lead pastor assignment. This move was very hard for our boys, who were in the 8th and 4th grades and had to leave behind a huge group of close friends. We were thrilled when our son was invited to a sleepover and took it as a sign that he was being accepted by the other adolescent boys.

In the wee hours of the morning, we got a phone call. He just said, "Dad, can you come pick me up?" That was it, no explanation. We were terrified. What happened? The boys were getting into their parent's alcohol cabinet and drinking. Our son told them that wasn't right and asked to be taken home. The host boy refused and said not to be a baby about it. Our son said if they wouldn't take him home, he wanted to call his dad to come pick him up. The host boy told him, "Sure, but you'll get in more trouble from waking up your dad to come and get you than just staying there." Our son told him that wouldn't be the case.

We had raised our son to know that there was NOTHING that would keep us from loving him—nothing! He could call us anytime—for any reason—and we would be there for him. We assured him that he had done the right thing and never discussed that night again.

God had the situation all in His hand. Those boys were bad news and never did accept him in their "group." God was protecting him during a difficult situation and steering him to a different path of friends. We are so glad we had taught him that it is okay to stand against the stream. He told us later how so alone he felt and how he hated that time of his life. He could have caved in or even rebelled against us, but he didn't. Thank you, Jesus for this strong-willed, independent boy.

Our son is now raising his own strong-willed son to be independent, and we continue to be proud of this young man. We are so blessed!

Prayer

Father, thank You for our children. You trusted us enough to raise them when we didn't have a clue how to do it. Thank You for helping us put our own pride on a back burner and listen to others who can help us when we cannot help ourselves. Thank You for Your Word that teaches us how to live and make wise choices. Thank You for loving us no matter what. We KNOW we can call on You at any time and You will be there. Thank You for those times when we choose to make unwise choices, because You will still be there. You are always there just waiting for us. Thank You for never forcing Yourself on us. You are so patient with us. As much as we love our children, You love them so much more. We are so blessed. Thank You, Jesus.

Trust, Hope, and Love

Lezlie Kraemer
Illinois District

"Trust steadily in God, hope unswervingly; love
extravagantly. And the best of the three is love."
1 CORINTHIANS 13:13 (MSG)

Our first assignment was a little rural church in western North Dakota.
The congregation of 18 included six of us Kraemers! Little did I know
back then how our children would grow to love the church so much.

As our first district assembly approached, I made up my mind that I was
not going. My list of reasons was long. After all, our four boys did not
have "good" church clothes. Their jeans were full of rips and holes at a
time when rips and holes were not cool. The meal allowance the church
provided was not nearly enough to feed our family for an entire week.
To top it off, the boys needed new shoes. Our son Kelly's tennis shoes
were so bad we had to use white athletic tape to keep the sole attached.
However, my argument did not fly with Kraemer. We were ALL going!

The trip started off with an ill-advised lunch at Pizza Hut that cost
more than half of our food allowance for the entire week. Once we
arrived at the church, I wanted to sit in the back, but Kraemer headed
to the front pew.

Church began and our DS's wife, Judy Bailey, sat down next to our clan.
Our son Kelly was so excited to sit by her. All of a sudden, he crossed
his leg at the knee and began bouncing his foot into the air, flapping
his shoe to the beat of the music. The tape that was holding the shoe
together began to unravel, and he must have challenged himself to keep
flapping it until it came completely apart.

To make things worse, the song evangelist called for volunteers to come up and sing. Scot, only four at the time, had slipped out from the pew and ran up to the choir before I could catch him. He could barely see over the choir altar, but he sure enjoyed the view he had from the front.

Our week at assembly was just the beginning of our love and walk with the church. We made the meal allowance stretch. The church services were heart changing. The boys had a blast staying in a hotel and making friends with other PKs. Kraemer gave his pastor's report, and I think I made it through the assembly with all my scruples still intact. All our boys came home with new shoes and clothes bought by a wonderful, caring laymen.

The church has always been so good to our family. I recently asked my grown children to tell me the things they loved about the church and growing up in the parsonage. Here are just a few of their responses:

- I always appreciated how my parents never spilled the beans on some of the ugly stuff that took place in the church. I think that helped us tremendously have a positive view of church. I now realize there can be headaches in the church, too, but not to dwell on them.

- There were no expectations put on us because we were in a parsonage. We had great churches full of great people and I think because our parents were so relational, it was fun to be a part of the church. Because they loved people, it was fun sharing life with them.

- We were so poor we got free lunches at school. HA!

- We got to attend camps, stay in hotels during conventions, and travel! We had the privilege of attending district and general conventions. We turned them into family vacations and great memories.

- Being remembered with Christmas and birthday gifts.

- We learned to trust Him. We did not have a lot and we saw our parents' faith lived out in front of us.

- I came to know many different kinds of people because of my parents and other church people. The people we met had different kinds of problems, different levels of education, different temperaments, and job statuses, and I think that has helped me work with them inside the church and out in the world.

- I have learned to love others from church laymen living it out before me in our churches. I still have the greatest friends because of the churches where my parents served.

Prayer

Thank You, Lord, for the churches You have given my family to serve. Has it always been rainbows, glitter, and unicorns everywhere? No way. But this one thing I do know—it has been a rock for us to build our house on. And my prayer for our children regarding the church is that may they always trust steadily in God, hope unswervingly, love extravagantly. And the best of these ... to love!

Never Stop

Mona Kunselman
Northwestern Ohio District

"I wait for the Lord, my whole being waits,
and in his word I put my hope."
PSALM 130:5

Christ's unconditional love for us models how we can love and pray for our children. We cannot beat ourselves up over the past by saying, "What if…" or "If only…" The truth is that our children have free will. They must decide for themselves to serve God. The heartbreaking question we ask at times is "Where did I go wrong?" The fact is that yes, we were not perfect parents, but we cannot control our children's decisions. Most of us tried to make every effort for our kids to be influenced by godly people and grow up listening to the Gospel message. We thought that those experiences would make them Christians. Yet salvation through Christ still comes down to a decision.

I want to give unconditional love to my child regardless of where he is spiritually. My desire is to love him like Christ loves me.

I pray the Holy Spirit will use life experiences to lead my child into a relationship with Christ. Let my prayer be "Holy Spirit, have Your way in reaching my child."

So let us not give up but keep diligently praying, knowing the Holy Spirit will work in ways we cannot. God does love our children unconditionally.

Prayer

In my time with You, You remind me that I did many things right in raising my child. Yet the voice inside me may still say I did not convince my child that following You was a great way to live. I continue to rest in the fact that my prayers are making a difference even though I do not see changes. I love my child, but You love him even more. Help me trust You in faith and believe that You have heard my prayers, You have seen my tears, and You will answer. Amen.

Thoughts on Praying for Our Children

Lisa Lacher
New Mexico District

"Rejoice always, pray continually, give thanks in all
circumstances; for this is God's will for you in Christ Jesus."
1 THESSALONIANS 5:16-18

Prayer is the constant, moment by moment, continual conversation with God that never ends. Jesus lived His life in this way. We are promised we can also.

At this moment in time, we all are struggling with what the new normal is to be. We are asked not to venture outside our doors, to stop all activities that make our day normal. We are making a way to work and care for our children in other than comfortable means. By the time you read this, my prayer is that COVID-19 has been slowed or stopped and our daily lives have maybe returned to normalcy.

In all the years Larry and I were raising our children, there were occasional periods where we found ourselves out of the routine, stretching ourselves as thin as possible. I would always pray for my children to learn to "go with the flow." There are new challenges each day and to be productive adults, one needs to be fluid. Each of us must be able to adjust for what is coming our way. Maintaining a continuous pattern of talking to God for direction and guidance is a truly vital part of our Christian walk.

I found myself praying consistently that our children would not get hurt in sports, not forget their lines during the plays, remember their test answers, and to always know, no matter what, their parents loved them beyond all else. I prayed my children would find spouses that knew the

Lord and walked with Him. I prayed that they would each find a personal relationship with Jesus.

I prayed that the church building would remain standing when our children were old enough to begin playing at church. Our children broke out windows and made holes in the walls. We would fix them and off they would go to keep playing. I prayed that they would find a home in each church we were pastoring, that God and love would reside there. No matter what came their way, Jesus had to be the one to follow.

On a Sunday morning in one church, when our children were four, five, and six, Larry had opened an altar call. Our six-year-old daughter responded to the call and began praying at the altar. I went and joined her, such a precious moment for a mom. After the service, an older woman came to me and said, "Children do not belong at the altar. They do not understand what they are doing." Who will teach them, if not their parents, that God hears every prayer from His children? Needless to say, no one ever knew that conversation took place, and our children have always found their place at the altar.

Whatever the new normal that has emerged from the pandemic of 2020, it must contain the daily, hourly, minute-by-minute prayers of parents for their children. Even when they are grown, the prayers continue, and we have added our grandchildren to the mix, for who will pray for them if not us?

Prayer

Dear Heavenly Father, what a role You have blessed us with as parents! The only manual is Your word, which is enough for all our needs. There are times when we do not have the words to pray, but thankfully You hear the words not spoken. Jesus, we lift our children and grandchildren to You, that You cover them under Your wing, that You place Your armor around them, protect them from the evils of our day. Raise them up to be Your children in their workplaces and homes, so that for generations upon generations You are their rock and salvation and the hearer of their prayers. Amen.

A Great Big Wonderful God

Beth Layton
West Virginia South District

> "I praise you because you made me in an amazing and wonderful
> way. What you have done is wonderful. I know this very well."
> PSALM 139:14 (NCV)

Isn't it wonderful to realize that God made each of us on purpose? Because He made us on purpose, we are not an accident or even an incident. Because of that, each of us is a gift to the world in general and an even greater gift to the specific people in "our world." Each of us is a divine work of art, signed by Almighty God Himself.

In the grander scheme of things, we human beings are not all that unique. We are not the only creatures with blood and hearts and flesh and hair. What makes us special is His image stamped on us to do good deeds. We are special and unique, not because of what we do or what we look like but because of whose we are and because of who made us.

The Bibles says in Ephesians 2:10… "God has made us what we are. In Christ Jesus, God made us to do good works, which God planned in advance for us to live our lives doing" (NCV).

As I think of my children and grandchildren today, I am profoundly reminded that they are God's gifts to me and to others and that they have a purpose because God made them on purpose.

That amazes me! And it motivates me to pray for them all the more, to pray that they will see and realize what I already know, that each of them is a gift and has a purpose.

Prayer

Father, thank You for making each of us so wonderfully. Thank You for the unique gift that we all are to each other. May all of our children and grandchildren come to realize how special they really are. And may they begin or continue to see Your great purpose for each of their lives. Amen.

The Mercies of God

Sandra Lopez
Southwest Latin American District

God's "mercies are new every morning."
LAMENTATIONS 3:23

I praise God for His continued mercy on my husband, daughters, and grandchildren. In Lamentations, God tells us that "His mercies are new every morning."

God gave us the privilege of having three daughters. My middle daughter, Sandra, is a woman whom God has blessed with many talents. She is a compassionate, friendly, caring woman, and when able, she always tries to help others.

I remember one occasion when we crossed the border from Tijuana, Mexico, to San Diego, California, Sandra saw a man walking barefoot. Suddenly I heard her voice saying, "Dad, can you give me your shoes so I can give them to that man who doesn't have shoes? It's too hot and the floor is burning his feet; you have more pairs of shoes at home." My husband answered, "If you are willing to get down and give them to him, I will." Sandra did not think twice; she got out of the car and gave the shoes to the man. That is just one of the many qualities my daughter Sandra possesses.

My husband and I pray for Sandra continually. She walked away from God's ways long ago. She suffers from anxiety, and lately she was diagnosed with heart complications. I have accepted the fact that my daughter is lost and she needs the constant mercies of God.

Prayer

Father in heaven, I ask You to bow Your ear at the request of Your children, Benjamin and Sandra. Please bring an inner healing into the heart of our daughter Sandra. Help her to accept Jesus as her personal Savior, for there is no better way than His. Father, forgive the sins of her youth, and may Your loving face shine and have mercy on her. Father, continue to take care of our daughter wherever she goes. In Thy name I pray, amen.

Dad, Mom, Where Are You?

Janet Lutz
East Ohio District

"The Lord himself goes before you and will be with you; he will never leave you nor forsake you. Do not be afraid; do not be discouraged."
DEUTERONOMY 31:8

"Mom! Where are you?!"

This is what I heard on the other end as I picked up the phone on a very busy Monday morning at the municipal court where I worked. Rachel was filled with panic and fear as she began to tell me she just got in a car accident on the busy Highway 75 as she headed back to study at the University of Findlay. She said she tried to call her dad but he didn't pick up. I told her I was so sorry as he was in a meeting all morning and probably wasn't looking at his phone. What was louder than her words was the tone of her voice. She sounded helpless, panicked, and alone. "Rachel, it's going to be okay. While Dad and I are not there at this moment, you are not all by yourself. We are coming to be with you."

As I spoke those words, I wondered how often I sound like this to my Heavenly Father. In stressful times, I, too, am impatient, feel alone, and wonder if God is paying attention to me. Sometimes, I cry out, "Lord, are you really listening to me? Where are you?"

In stressful times, I sometimes doubt God's goodness and His presence being with me. In Deuteronomy 31, the Israelites did too. They were preparing to enter the Promised Land knowing their leader, Moses, would stay behind. Moses reassured them and reminded his people, "The Lord himself goes before you and will be with you; he will never leave you nor forsake you. Do not be afraid; do not be discouraged."

That promise, that God is always with us, remains a cornerstone of our faith today.

Where is God? He is right here, right now, right with us, always ready to hear our prayers.

Prayer

Dear Heavenly Father, when I fail to trust You and lean on You for guidance and direction, please forgive me. Please remind me to trust You, for You are good and want only the best for me. I know You will never leave me nor forsake me. Thank You for Your promise and for Your love to me. Thank You for hearing my prayer!

A Hole in 37

Elaine Mahaffey
Southwestern Ohio District

"Blessed is the one who perseveres under trial because,
having stood the test, that person will receive the crown of
life that the Lord has promised to those who love him."
JAMES 1:12

Grandchildren teach us wonderful life lessons. In fact, I have learned a lot from our grandkids! Emily has been my teacher on several occasions. She is very determined and, sometimes, even stubborn. We have seen these traits in her, especially in the following story.

One evening, the family went to play putt-putt golf. This was a new challenge to Emily—she had never played putt-putt golf before, but she knew the basic premise of the game is to get the ball in the hole.

Different family members began rising to the challenge. Mom Bethany, dad Kevin, and older sister Madelyn all sunk the ball in 3, 4, or 5 tries, earning respectable scores at a par three putt-putt course. Emily's turn came at last. She soon realized that the goal was not as accessible as it looked, but being the determined little girl that she is, she kept trying.

Bethany said they all painstakingly watched as Emily re-seated her ball repeatedly. Bethany began counting. They encouraged Emily to move on to the next hole, but she would not quit. Finally, after 37 tries, the ball plopped into the cup! A true celebration followed! Determination had paid off. It didn't matter that it had taken Emily 37 tries. The important thing was that she had accomplished the task.

As adults, how often do we give up trying? We quit because of personal frustration or embarrassment among peers or lack of confidence because of past failures. We limit ourselves by quitting too soon perhaps thinking that success should come easily. Why waste time failing? Move on to things that make us look successful. After all, "success" is the name of the game in our 21st century culture!

Emily's example has spoken to me. In my breast cancer battle, I could have given up many times. Who wants to live in pain? Who wants to live with side effects from chemotherapy? Who wants to live with a tumor in the leg, unable to walk, or with a right hand that has lost all sense of feeling from lymphedema or neuropathy from chemotherapy? Not me!

This story emphasizes the importance of persistent prayer. Each month, as we see the names of children that we are praying for, I believe that through our persistence and faithfulness to lift these precious souls to God, He hears these prayers and He will work in their lives. We may pray 37 months, 137 months, or more... but God is faithful!

God's Word tells us in James 1:12, "Blessed is the one who perseveres under trial because, having stood the test, that person will receive the crown of life that the Lord has promised to those who love him."

And in James 5:16, "The prayer of a righteous person is powerful and effective."

We need to celebrate the victories of a "hole in 37" and not give up while trying. We need to learn from Emily. God wants us to persevere, and the celebration will be sweet!

Prayer

Father, in times that seem so difficult or unbearable, let us keep our eyes on You. Let us push through with perseverance and not give up. When things seem to not be in our favor, when days seem long and difficult, help us focus on the goal. We are thankful for who You are and the strength only You can give. Whether it be a difficult job situation, a relationship, failing health, or a loss, continue to encourage us and comfort us. You are faithful, Father. Amen.

Intervention and Intercession

Elaine Mason
North Carolina District

"I urge, then, first of all, that petitions, prayers, intercession and thanksgiving be made for all people—for kings and all those in authority, that we may live peaceful and quiet lives in all godliness and holiness. This is good, and pleases God our Savior, who wants all people to be saved and to come to a knowledge of the truth."

1 TIMOTHY 2:1-4

I grew up in a home of five children. My two oldest siblings were a half-sister and half-brother. Their birth mother was killed in a car accident when they were very small. My mother and father married and had three kids. Before long, our dad left us for another family, leaving our mother with five kids. You can imagine the trauma, difficulty, and sadness in our home. Thankfully, we had Christian aunts and uncles who took care of us and prayed for us.

We lived down the alley from a Church of the Nazarene. In our teens, my brother became friends with the pastor's daughter and started hanging out at the parsonage. Soon, he began visiting the church. Later, my older brother visited as well and got saved at a city-wide crusade that the church helped sponsor. It wasn't long before they invited me to attend. At a fall revival service, I gave my heart to Jesus.

One by one, the church touched my family. The people loved us, cared for us, and took us under their wing. They modeled faith, love, and holiness for us in ways that we had seldom, if ever, seen. They gave us a place to find hope and healing. They gave us a family of fellowship and a place to serve. Before all was said and done, all five of us Flack children ended up being influenced and touched by the church down the street.

The Bible says in Romans 8 that Jesus makes intercession for us, but He also intervenes for us.

Jesus consistently walks into the most difficult, depressing, and desperate situations to bring salvation, hope, and life. He walked into the life of a Samaritan woman, a leper, a blind man, a little tax collector, and twelve disciples.

Prayers of intercession for our loved ones and friends is an important ministry—perhaps one of the most important things we can do. To call on the God of heaven to love and care for those that we care about and to join others in this work is vital. We invite others to pray for our children, our parents, and our grandkids because we want them to be saved, healed, or helped.

But those for whom we intercede also need us to intervene. Many of them need Jesus to walk into their lives in our flesh. They need to see Jesus in the tangible, visible acts of love and kindness, generosity and compassion, in the attitudes, behaviors, and actions of the church body.

There is a song that says, "He's Ever Interceding." Yes, He is, but I am glad that He is ever seeking to save that which is lost; He is ever intervening.

Prayer

Father in Heaven, thank You for the gift of your Son Jesus, who now sits at Your right hand and intercedes for us. We know He intercedes for those we love. As a great high priest, He mediates between all men and the God of heaven.

And God, we pray that through the Holy Spirit and through Spirit-filled followers, the Lord Jesus will also intervene in those lives. May the broken, the lost, the least, the disheartened, and the desperate know the power of a Savior who walks into their mess and offers grace, forgiveness, and healing.

We thank You for the prevenient grace of Jesus that entered our arena and impressed upon us the love of the Trinity and convinced us that the death and resurrection of Jesus were the means by which we might become the children of God.

Help us, O Lord, to be people who not only intercede but intervene in the lives of those for whom Jesus died. Amen.

A Psalm in Times of Fears

Linda McCann
Canada Pacific District

"The Lord is my shepherd."
PSALM 23

When my children were young, there was an outbreak of fear. It was at the time of 9/11 when the world—especially the USA—felt vulnerable.

I remember turning my children's hearts and minds to Psalm 23: The Shepherd's Psalm. I also prepared several weeks of activities for our children's church to memorize this psalm so that my children and others could be comforted in this "new reality."

It seems that we are now in a new "new reality." We are learning to live in the midst of a pandemic.

COVID-19 seems so powerful as it attacks the most vulnerable among us. Many may feel that they are "walking through the valley of the shadow of death" (v. 4). And yet, the Lord is still our Shepherd.

I once heard the story of a boy who discovered this promise and took it to heart. High on the moors in the Welsh highlands, two ministers met a young shepherd boy who had impaired hearing and was illiterate. They explained that Jesus wanted to be his shepherd, who would always look after him just like the boy looked after his sheep. They taught him to repeat the words "The Lord is my shepherd" (Psalm 23:1) using the fingers and thumb of his right hand to help him remember, starting with his thumb and then a finger for each word. They told him to pause at the fourth word "my" and remember "this psalm was meant for me."

Some years later, one of them happened to pass through that same village and asked after the shepherd boy. The previous winter there had been terrible storms, and the boy had died on the hills, buried in a snowdrift. The villager who was telling the story said, "There was one thing, however, that we didn't understand. When his body was discovered, he was holding the fourth finger of his right hand."

This is what we can teach to and pray over our children and grandchildren: that God wants to be our God, that He wants to be our protector and caregiver, that His promises are personal, that we can have Him as our Shepherd, that this psalm is meant for us.

No matter how we are retraining ourselves to live in this new reality, let's spend time praying for each other. Let us spend time praying that our children and grandchildren will be comforted by the fact that God is a good Shepherd and that He will always be their Shepherd as they choose to be His "sheep." And let us, who have walked beside quiet waters and in paths of righteousness as well as in valleys of the shadow of death and in the presence of our enemies, remind those who are "lambs" in age and in the faith that He leads, restores, and guides continually... all the days of our life until we dwell with Him forever.

Prayer

Dear Shepherd, thank You for guiding and protecting us and the lambs we love through all of the various circumstances of our lives. Help us to trust You continually, even when we are on uncertain paths. Remind us of Your presence. Thank You that You are our Shepherd always. Amen.

Our Eyes Are on Him

Karla McCormick
East Tennessee District

"For we have no power to face this vast army that is attacking
us. We do not know what to do, but our eyes are on you."
2 CHRONICLES 20:12

The year was 1973. Watergate was in full swing. One month prior to the Saturday Night Massacre, Ron and I joined the ranks of parenthood. Our beautiful little boy entered the world of two young adults who had no idea what it meant to raise a child. We were 4,621 miles from home, living in the German economy.

Most of our friends, including commissioned army officers, were leaving, no longer able to live on the devalued dollar. There were days when we literally sifted through the crevices of our living room furniture to find coins to buy baby food. However, we had determined early on to pay our tithes and trust God for the outcome. There were nights when raging fevers threatened our little boy while two trusting parents prayed, "For we have no power to face this vast army that is attacking us. We do not know what to do, but our eyes are on you" (2 Chronicles 20:12).

Those early days of forced-complete trust should have been a forever reminder of the faithfulness of God in every situation. I am sad to say that has not been the case. Our grandson Austin used to sit in the backseat singing "I Exalt Thee" at the top of his voice. It sounded more like, "I exhaust thee, I exhaust thee, I exhaust thee, Oh Lord!"

I am so thankful for the promise of Isaiah 40:28: "Do you not know? Have you not heard? The LORD is the everlasting God, the Creator of the ends of the earth. He will not grow tired or weary, and his understanding no one can fathom."

Time and time again, situation after situation, child after child, and grandchild after grandchild, our Heavenly Father has proven Himself more than enough.

We do not know what to do, but our eyes are on You.

Prayer

Father, we are reminded once again that in those moments when we do not know what to do or even how to pray, we can trust You completely. How thankful we are that You do not grow weary in proving Your love and care for us time and time again. Help us to be keenly aware that Your ways are higher than our ways and Your thoughts much higher than our thoughts. Help us to keep our eyes upon You and quickly give You the praise when the impossible is made possible. To the One who was and is and is to come, we pray! Amen.

Lessons in the Waiting

Denice McKain
Chicago Central District

"But hope that is seen is no hope at all. Who hopes
for what they already have? But if we hope for what
we do not yet have, we wait for it patiently."
ROMANS 8:24-25

I sat in my car, dazed at the sight of my daughter returning to her old life. She had ended up in a dangerous place and had come to live with us. There were some positive moments as she gradually regained a semblance of stability, but along the way, her spirit toward us changed and things ended on a disappointing and very painful note. That was over three years ago, and we remain a fractured family.

As parents, how do we make sense of these experiences? So many questions whirl around in our minds: "How could I have messed up my daughter so much?" "Why do other people seem to have trouble-free lives and great family relationships?"

In reflecting on my situation, it became clear that most lessons are learned in the waiting when we don't know how to pray but are trusting that God is working behind the scenes. Here are five simple lessons I am learning.

1. Listen to the right voice! As long as we are in this fleshly body, we will have tempting thoughts of condemnation. But do we have to accept them? By all means, NO! Do those thoughts come from God? By all means, NO! Those thoughts do not come from God. He is our Shepherd, and we have to train ourselves to listen to His voice (John 10:27). As we come to know His voice more intimately,

we must "take captive every thought to make it obedient to Christ!" (2 Corinthians 10:5). The Holy Spirit gently convicts. The enemy of our soul condemns. We must be militant regarding the thoughts we allow because we only have so much emotional capacity. Being lax in this area will sap our spirits and drain us emotionally.

2. Avoid the comparison trap! God has us all on a unique path, and we need to steadfastly follow Him, "throwing off everything that hinders and the sin that so easily entangles" (Hebrews 12:1). The comparison trap is nothing new. Look no further than Peter in His interaction with the risen Jesus. After Jesus had asked him three times to "feed my sheep," Peter pointed to John and said, "Lord, what about him?" Jesus admonished him by saying, "If I want him to remain alive until I return, what is that to you? You must follow me" (John 21:19). Time spent dwelling on how things are going better for other families is time taken away from following Jesus!

3. Be willing to share your painful situation with others. I have been so blessed by our brave sisters in Christ who have shared some deeply painful things from their past. Sharing our pain with others and enjoying their intercession for us is so liberating. The enemy is cast out when we confess to each other and pray for one another so that "you may be healed!" (James 5:16). When you don't have the strength to pray fervently, isn't it nice to know that there are others "standing in the gap" for us, including Jesus who is "at the right hand of God, interceding for us" (Roman 8:34)?

4. Rejoice that God is enlarging your capacity for empathizing with others. We make so many assumptions about people having pain-free lives. This is a myth. Everyone has challenges yet might wonder if anyone understands his or her unique situation. God may have just prepared you to meet that very need! The Scripture says, "the God of all comfort, who comforts us in all our troubles, so that we can comfort those in any trouble with the comfort we ourselves receive from God" (2 Corinthians 1:4). None of us enjoys the pain, but God never "wastes it"!

5. And finally, don't be ashamed to get any and all the help you need… physically, emotionally, mentally, and even medically during and after

painful times. I am not a doctor, but I know personally that extreme stress causes our bodies and brains to be sapped of needed chemicals to function properly. I am not discounting the prominent place of faith, only saying that God uses many methods for our healing.

While we are waiting and hoping for what we do not yet have, let us not forget that God is working as much in us as He is in the loved ones we are praying for, especially our prodigal children! Praise His Name!

Prayer

Heavenly Father, help us to steadfastly follow You, looking not to the left or right but at the path You have set before us, knowing that while we hope and wait for what we do not yet have, You are working not only in the lives of those we love but in our lives as well to accomplish Your will. Thank You. In Jesus' name, amen!

Mercy and Blueberry Pancakes

Gloria McKellips
Northeast Oklahoma District

> "But he said to me, 'My grace is sufficient for you,
> for my power is made perfect in weakness.'"
> **2 CORINTHIANS 12:9a**

We recently visited our family in Texas for a short, 24-hour trip. The morning of that trip, we all sat down to eat some wonderful breakfast tacos our daughter had picked up, and most of us were joyfully anticipating the good food.

Our "Little E," however, was the exception. From the moment we sat down, she made it clear that she was not interested in the tacos. She only wanted "booberry" pancakes. Her mother kindly let her know that we were having breakfast tacos that day. Little E continued to resist; she began to whine and cry, and after a while, her mom decided she needed a time out.

Little E went to her room crying. The door was shut, but we could still hear her anguish over not having blueberry pancakes.

The crying began to stop. Little E eventually made her way back to the table. Her mother hugged her and asked if she had something to say to everyone. Eventually, with that tiny little voice, the words "I'm sorry" came out amidst some lingering sniffles.

She paused, looked up at her mom, and then stated, "but I still want booberry pancakes." She tried hard not to whine and cry, knowing it could mean another trip to her room.

We all tried to hide our smiles while her parents glanced at each other as they tried to figure out how to respond to Little E's plea. Our daughter then spoke these words to her sweet child.

"Thank you for apologizing to everyone." Long pause. "Little E, do you deserve blueberry pancakes?"

"No, mommy."

"I'm going to give you blueberry pancakes. But what is it called, Little E, when you get what you don't deserve?"

Little E tried hard not to cry as she quietly said, "Gwace, mommy, it's gwaaaace!"

It was a powerful moment for me. Grateful tears began to roll down my cheeks. I was grateful for parents who choose to teach their children through tough moments, grateful for God's unmerited favor in my own life and how it has permeated my daily routines, relationships, and family, and grateful as God spoke to me immediately through this visual lesson with the faces of those I was struggling to give grace to.

Prayer

Father, forgive me when I have not recognized Your grace in the midst of my self-centered days. Help me to remember the high cost You paid for me to receive forgiveness, grace, and love. Help me to be a person who offers forgiveness, love, and grace to others in return, even though it can be difficult. Thank You for Your faithful, powerful reminders amidst the simplest of moments. Thank You that Your grace really is sufficient. In Jesus' name, amen.

Praying for Our Children

Silvia Mena
Western Latin American District

"The Lord bless you and keep you; the Lord make his
face shine upon you and be gracious to you; the Lord
turn his face toward you and give you peace."
NUMBERS 6:24-26

We started praying for our children before they were born. After my first pregnancy resulted in a miscarriage, we prayed more fervently for a child. God answered our prayer and in December 1987, our son Emmanuel was born. After our son was born, we started praying for a daughter, and in June 1989, our daughter Melody was born. We always prayed for and with our children since they were babies. As they got older, we would pray with them and finish our praying time with this benediction.

"May the Lord bless you and keep you
May the Lord make His face to shine on you
And be gracious to you.
May the Lord lift up His face towards you
And give you peace."
Numbers 6:24-26

The prayers for our children have covered them in their infant years, through elementary school, junior high, high school, university, while choosing a spouse, and now as parents raising their own children in the grace and knowledge of our Lord Jesus Christ. God has been gracious to them, lifting His face towards them and giving them peace and joy. The Lord has kept them safe from harm. He has given them faith to rest on His unfailing arms. He has guided them in their daily walk and watched them through the night. He has given them strength for every task and hope that's always bright. He has given them joy of heart and peace of mind. The Lord has been very gracious to them.

Prayer

Thank You, God, for Your unfailing love and for Your promises
that never fail.

A Renewed Hope and Cheer

Julie Miller
Anaheim District

> "Lord, when doubt fills my mind, when my heart is in turmoil,
> quiet me and give me a renewed hope and cheer."
> **PSALM 94:19 (TLB)**

There isn't much in life that can give us more joy or cause us more pain than our children. We hold those tiny babies in our arms and maybe for the first time, we really fully comprehend God's love for us. There is nothing we would not do to protect them from harm. We look into their little faces and see hope for the future. We love them fiercely, like we have never loved before. And while we may feel inadequate in those first days and weeks, we figure it out because those precious babies depend on us for their very lives.

And then they start walking and talking, and it is so exciting! They are like little sponges, and we do everything we can to teach them about the world around them and about Jesus, who somehow loves them much more than we do!

And they continue to grow. They go to school. They get involved in sports and clubs. They listen to music and watch television and interact on social media. They spend time with friends. Other people have access into their lives. We continue to try to protect them and remind them that Jesus loves them, but it gets more difficult as they get older.

And then they become adults. Maybe they love Jesus. Maybe they don't. But they are adults, making their own choices, and we are torn between telling them what we think and possibly being rejected or respecting their decisions even though we can see that they are going to get hurt.

It's hard. And there are days when it can be emotionally so difficult that we don't even want to get out of bed.

Several years ago, we were going through some challenging stuff with our daughter. I was a wreck. It hurt, and there was nothing I could do but just watch it play out. It was hard. But in the midst of all that, a friend of mine gave me this scripture.

"Lord, when doubt fills my mind, when my heart is in turmoil, quiet me and give me a renewed hope and cheer." Psalm 94:19 (TLB)

My heart was in turmoil all the time. And I lived in the land of doubt and fear. So I wrote that verse on a little whiteboard and hung it over my desk at school. I read it several times a day. My friend had given me the verse for that specific situation, so my plan was to change that verse out every week or two depending on what God was saying to me.

It has been nine years since that time. The situation was resolved, but we still feel the effects of it on some days more than others. It changed us. We have mostly adjusted, but nine years later, that verse is still on my little whiteboard.

Life can be tough sometimes, really tough. And the enemy is good at trash talk. That makes quieting our minds a challenge! But no matter what is happening around us, God can give us a renewed hope and cheer...although we may have to work a bit at accessing it!

Prayer

Father, we have issues. You know we have issues because You know us! You created us to love our children with everything we have, and it is so hard to remember that You only give them to us for a short time! It hurts us when they hurt. It hurts us when they make questionable choices. It hurts us to see them reject You! We want to fix it. We want to say "Listen, here is what you need to do..." but since You gave us all free will, our adult kids get to make their own choices, and they don't have to listen to us! But we have to listen to You! So please help us remember that our children belong to You, wherever they are. Put people in their path will point them to You. Keep them safe. And when they are facing difficult consequences because of their choices, help us to stay out of the way and let You work! Quiet our minds. Help us to recognize Satan's trash talk for what it is! Give us joy even when we can't stop thinking about what is happening with our kids. Help us to trust You with that which is most precious to us. We love You, Jesus, and thank You for Your faithfulness in all things. In Your name we pray, amen!

Watching the Horizon

Melissa Mowry
Northwest District

"You, Lord, are forgiving and good, abounding
in love to all who call to You."
PSALM 86:5

"Dear Jesus, please come in to my tummy. Amen." I will never forget that sweet, sincere prayer of my three-year-old at home one afternoon. My two children had been asking me questions about Jesus. I answered the questions and was just getting ready to ask if they wanted me to lead them in prayer when one child started praying. The other child prayed as well, changing the wording slightly from "tummy" to "heart." I was overjoyed! They had prayed to receive Jesus of their own free will.

My husband and I started praying for both of our children even before they were born. We have prayed for many good things in their lives, but above all that they would love and follow the Lord. While they were growing up, we prayed with them and for them daily. We tried to teach our kids that being a Christian isn't about religion but relationship with our Savior, Jesus Christ.

Now, both of our children are young adults. One has chosen to follow Jesus and live for Him, but the other has chosen to walk away from Jesus and follow the ways of the world. Our hearts are broken, and we ask ourselves, "Why? How could this happen?"

The answer dates back to the beginning of time. God created a paradise for His children in the Garden of Eden where they could be in relationship with Him. God did not forcibly compel them to obey Him but gave them a choice. He gave them a free will.

Our free will is a gift that can prove our genuine love for God as we daily choose to live for Him. Unfortunately, that same free will can also be used to turn away from God and go our own way.

Jesus' story of the prodigal son is such a comfort to me. Surely the father's heart was broken as he watched his beloved son walk away to what he thought was freedom. Yet the father never gave up hope as he watched the horizon, ready to run to his son with an outpouring of grace when he returned from his wanderings.

Prayer

Lord, thank You that You don't give up on us, even when we use our free will to turn away. Please reach this child with Your love, truth, and grace. My hope is in You, and I will keep watching the horizon with You. Amen.

Holy Love

Pat Ottley
Canada Central District

"To act justly and to love mercy and to walk humbly with your God."
MICAH 6:8b

Are you experiencing crisis fatigue yet?

2020 promised to be an exciting year. After all, it's 2020—the start of a new decade. There were so many exciting things we were looking forward to this year! And then, the flood gates opened, bringing a global pandemic and unrest regarding racial issues with protests throughout the United States, Canada, and other countries around the world.

Has crisis fatigue settled in on you?

I can picture in my mind's eye Jesus standing up in the Temple Courts and saying to a sea of people who were crisis fatigued, "Anyone who is thirsty may come to me! Anyone who believes in me may come and drink! For the Scriptures declare, 'Rivers of living water will flow from his heart'" John 7:37-38 (NLT). These were Jews who were hopeless and harassed under the thumb of the Roman Empire. Talk about crisis! And Jesus says to them, COME—If you are thirsty, COME to Me.

So, if you are experiencing crisis fatigue, Jesus and His rest is available to all of us.

When we come to Him, He gives us His life-giving water that then flows from us to others. The rest that Jesus offers strips us of our anxieties and stress and prepares us to join Him in His mission. The overflow from Jesus that runs through our hearts toward those around us leads us, "To act justly and to love mercy and to walk humbly with your God" Micah 6:8b.

To act justly and to love mercy speaks to our responsibility to speak out for those who cannot do so for themselves. It speaks to all of us doing what is right.

To walk humbly with your God speaks to the attitude in which we do that. We must act justly and love mercy with the attitude that Christ Jesus had (Philippians 2:6-8).

To lash out with angry rhetoric or aggressive actions puts us in a category other than Christlike and at the least damages our testimony and the very message we proclaim. At worst, it disqualifies us from the call that Jesus extends for us to join Him in the ministry of reconciliation just as the Apostle Paul was concerned being disqualified for the prize in the race (1 Corinthians 9:27) if he did not submit himself daily to God.

Let us be careful to be Christlike in our actions and words. Let God's name be kept holy in our words and actions.

To all Christians, let us all "act justly and to love mercy and to walk humbly with your God." Let the prayer that Jesus taught us be lived out through us. Let our lives, empowered by the Holy Spirit, be for a thirsty and dying world, a foretaste of heaven, right here on earth. Let us show holy love in all we do and say.

Prayer

Our Father, who art in heaven,
hallowed be thy name;
thy kingdom come; thy will be done
on earth as it is in heaven.
Give us this day our daily bread;
and forgive us our trespasses
as we forgive those who trespass against us;
and lead us not into temptation,
but deliver us from evil. Amen.

Influencing Future Generations

Mary Palmer
Missouri District

"A good person leaves an inheritance for their children's children."
PROVERBS 13:22

I am grateful for the influence we can have in our family's lives through the power of prayer! From time to time, I am aware of the influence of the prayers of my maternal grandmother before she went to heaven. And, through the years, I have seen God's work in my family's lives as a result of my prayers. What an awesome privilege and opportunity we have to leave a spiritual inheritance for current and future generations through our prayers.

A while back, I was thinking about how quickly we disappear from the memory of future generations. Those just three or four generations ahead won't know or remember us. But we can still have an influence in their lives through the prayers we pray for them while we're living. I want those who come after me to experience the blessings of knowing and living for God, and I want to meet them in heaven someday.

I want to leave a spiritual heritage for my family through my life and prayers, both those who are alive now and those who will come after me.

Prayer

Father, thank You for the privilege and opportunity You give us to influence our families, especially through prayer, for generations to come. Help me to faithfully intercede and pray for those who will come after me. Thank You for Your love and faithfulness to us. In Jesus' name, amen.

Offers of Peace

Julie Poole
Georgia District

"Trust in the Lord with all your heart and
lean not on your own understanding."
PROVERBS 3:5

In the spring of 2000, I was driving home from a neighboring town with my two young sons. As we were traveling down the state highway, my car began to have trouble. I made it into our garage just as the car stopped for good.

While I was grateful to be home, I was VERY angry with the Lord. That was our only car. We had a very small salary, two small children, and no money in the bank. I took the boys inside, put them down for naps, and went to have a discussion with the Lord.

In the midst of beating my fists against His chest in frustration, He gently said, "go read Proverbs." I promptly told Him that Proverbs had nothing to do with my car and I did not want to read that right then. I continued my rant and He continued to say, "go read Proverbs."

This went on for a half hour or so. Thankfully, He is relentlessly patient with us. Since He would give me no other answers, I finally opened the Word to see how He was going to fix either my car or my bank account. I started with chapter 1 and made it to the first few verses of chapter 3 where He stopped me: "Trust in the Lord with all your heart, LEAN NOT ON YOUR OWN UNDERSTANDING." I knew He wanted me to hear that, but I just kept arguing that had nothing to do with my car!

As I sat there confused and trying to figure out the lesson (or solution), our home phone rang. It was Bob Broadbooks. He told me that he would like Kyle to give him a call about a church. I thanked him and let him know I would pass along the message. I went back to my chair and prayer. I told the Lord that we could not move; we hadn't lived there long enough. It didn't seem fair to the church to leave during good days of growth when we had been there such a short time. Well, to make this long story a little shorter, the Lord spent the next couple of months teaching me that sometimes my own understanding—even when it's with good intentions and love for His people—is not the same as His plan and His way. And, you guessed it, we moved.

Within just a few months of moving, our 4-year-old son began having severe, intermittent neck pain. It was debilitating when it hit. Over several months, we went to multiple doctors who told us there was nothing wrong with him. But the pain and tears continued. Then we found the right doctors who did the right tests and discovered that he had a congenital condition called a Chiari malformation that would require surgery on his skull. The good news was that he had not developed any syrinx, which can cause nerve damage to hands and feet and sometimes lead to paralysis. During prayer the next day, the Lord told me He had this situation under control and specifically offered peace to me. I simply had to take it. He also revealed that this was part of His plan for us to move. That pastorate that I had insisted we shouldn't leave was out in the country too far from medical treatment, and we would not have pursued these doctors for help.

We prayed and our people prayed over our boy during surgery and the days that followed. His recovery was quicker than the doctors had expected, and he was back to normal before we knew it. He still has a scar down the back of his neck that looks like a zipper. Every time I see it or hear him play his guitar (with fingers that weren't damaged from a syrinx), I am reminded of the Lord's faithfulness. I rejoice that He taught me, through prayer, to trust His plan, to accept the peace He offers, and that my obedience brings blessings I cannot foresee.

Prayer

Father, remind us that Your faithfulness is not a thing of the past. Your Word teaches us that You are always faithful as You go before us, walk beside us, and protect us from behind. Help us to accept Your peace, knowing that Your ways are higher and that You have our situations under control. Give us the strength to obey, even when we don't understand the why or the how. You are ever faithful, Lord! We choose You and Your ways.

A Jealous Mother

Toni Porter
General Superintendent Spouse

"And we know that in all things God works for the good of those
who love him, who have been called according to his purpose."
ROMANS 8:28

Our son Bill was in sixth grade. He came home from school and told me that he was running for class president. His opponent was a popular boy who I knew would be a good candidate for this office. Being a "jealous" mother who wanted her son to win the election, I got on my knees and prayed that Bill would win the election. Nevertheless, being a "spiritual" mother, I added, "Not my will but Your will be done, Lord!"

I vacillated all day between my will and God's will as I impatiently waited for my son to return from school. When Bill walked into the house, my immediate question was, "Who won the election for class president?" To my great surprise, he named a girl! Bill had been elected as vice-president. The other boy had declined the office. Bill was the only boy on an all-girl council!

I started to laugh! God had shown me that prayer could be funny. And even when our desire and will are so stubbornly strong, the Lord can gently guide us to His will and make everything work together for good.

What was my part in my son's vice-presidency? Every Friday, I had to make chocolate chip cookies that were sold for class projects. Being missionaries in Guatemala where it was hard to obtain chocolate chips, I used half the chocolate chips the recipe called for… and they still tasted very good, and the class made a lot of money.

It is good to remember God's faithfulness when we prayed for our children in their younger years. God was working all things for their good in their lives through our prayers. And today, He continues to hear and answer our prayers for our richest rewards.

"In the same way your Father in heaven is not willing that any of these little ones should perish." Matthew 18:14

Our richest rewards will always be His and our "little ones."

Prayer

Dear Jesus, we mothers think our children are the most special. Help us to be patient when our children are not the smartest, the most attractive, or when they have not chosen to follow You. Help us to be mothers who pray, love, nurture, and forgive. Children are gifts. Amen.

The Song

Vicki Power
Hawaii Pacific District

"Surely your goodness and love will follow me all the days of
my life, and I will dwell in the house of the Lord forever."
PSALM 23:6

My upbringing shaped my view of prayer. My mom often prayed quietly in her room. For a period of time, she fasted one day each week to pray especially for the persons her daughters might marry. A few weeks before she died, she told me she was so thankful that we were both in happy marriages. Her prayers were not like fairy dust sprinkled over our lives to make everything happy ever after. They have been effective in how we move through our lives—how we see, how we live, and how we love.

Rick and I had flown to the Kona Coast of the Big Island to enjoy a few nights away from home. The setting was peaceful with a beautiful green lawn extending out toward the wide, blue ocean. Shortly after we arrived, we received a call that required me to return home early to be with our young-adult daughter. She was like a wounded bird. Hers was a beautiful song muted by a dark night over which she had no control.

We had been encouraged by signs of mercy and healing along the way, but this seemed like a setback. I was discouraged and questioning in prayer. It was just before sunset at the resort, and I heard a familiar tune. The song became clearer and my soul grew quiet. Standing on the edge of the great lawn, facing the ocean, was a man playing "Amazing Grace" on bagpipes. There were no other people around. I listened with reverent hope. Kona sunsets are magnificent anytime, but the added sound of "Amazing Grace" hovering over the water was a gift to my perspective.

The next day, back home with our daughter, we went for lunch at a seaside place where we could talk. With my soul quieted by the beauty of the hymn, I was able to give less advice and listen more. By listening with understanding love and watching with hope, we began to hear our wounded bird sing again. The privilege of prayer calms my soul and clears my vision.

This morning, many years after the event I just described, I'll get to be with our granddaughter, River Jean. We will hear a chorus of birdsong in the trees and walk to the ocean where we will play together in small and gentle waves. The sounds and message of "Amazing Grace" are never far from my heart.

Prayer

Father, thank You for the beauty of this day. Thank You for Your goodness and mercy. Thank You for those who love me and those You have given me to love. Thank You for Your sustaining, connecting, amazing grace. May we live near the sea of joy and rest under trees of peace. In the name of the One who created all things, amen.

God's Story in Jen's Life: Mom's Version

Joan Read
Canada Quebec District

"For his anger lasts only a moment, but his favor lasts a lifetime;
weeping may stay for the night, but rejoicing comes in the morning."
PSALM 30:5

Unlike Jen, I didn't keep a journal during those dark days. I wanted to block them out, not preserve them for memoirs!

In her teens, Jen began rebelling toward family, faith, and everything we held dear. She refused to even close her eyes as we prayed at meals and used poisonous adjectives to describe me on the phone to her friends. Who taught her to smoke? And how did she become an alcoholic?

We tried "tough love," psychologists, counselors, and educational plans. Our last hope was sending her away to the Dominican Republic to attend a private Christian school for troubled kids. We contacted the school and got all the paper work together. Jen didn't know that the battery of tests and doctor visits were part of the admission process for a school far away from home. We were desperate.

Jen's therapist very reluctantly agreed to our plan. Jen would have to make a choice: put herself back under our authority and obey our house rules or be shipped off to the school in the DR. "We must tell her together in my office," the therapist said. We made the appointment to do just that. Meanwhile, Jen began the "week from hell" with an evening out with a friend. Hours later, when I realized she wasn't coming home, I called her friend. She sounded very calm when she told me that our precious daughter had gone off from the party with some boys. She didn't know where, but added, "If they weren't nice guys, I wouldn't have let her go!" Once again, I fell to my knees at the side of my bed, a place already soggy with my desperate tears, and cried out to God for His mercy! "Please, please, please protect Jen! Bring her home. Save her!" I was there most of the night.

That week was a nightmare. There were several household disasters, including a fire in the kitchen, a hole in the linoleum floor, and a flood in the upstairs laundry. Finally, while I was mindlessly, furiously cleaning the venetian blind in Jen's room, my hand slipped and I sliced right through the thin metal slats. I declared, "That's it! I recognize you, Satan! You've gone one step too far. You have no business in this family. You're out of here!" Jen called sometime in the middle of that week and calmly said, "Don't worry, Mom." She told us she was in Topeka but wouldn't say where. At a loss for words, I blurted out, "You already missed a dental appointment (as if that even really mattered when her very life was at stake) and you have a therapy appointment this Friday." She told me she would be there. That was it! The only glimpse of hope we had.

The day came and Terry stayed home in case Jen showed up. When I arrived at the therapist's office, I found Ben, Jen's 19-year-old boyfriend, in the waiting room. I could tell he was uncomfortable, agitated. We sat a few minutes until the therapist opened her door and invited me in.

Jen was dressed in her typical black clothes and chain jewelry, eyes black with mascara, but her face was changed. There was a light, a gentle smile.

Jen softly spoke, "I'm sorry Mom! And I told God I'm sorry too." We hugged; we cried; we laughed. Jen had come into the office totally desperate, "at the bottom." The place we both feared and prayed for had come, and Jen was transformed!

Terry wouldn't believe when I called to tell him about our meeting. He didn't believe it until Jen got home and asked to paint her room periwinkle! She wanted to replace the dark art, terrible faces, daggers, and doom with light! There's more to this initial transformation in Jen's life, but for now, know that I am praying with you as you wait and pray for your prodigal to come home!

Prayer

Father, please answer every prayer to save our children. Redeem every attempt of the enemy to rob them of the sweet relationship with Jesus! In His name, amen.

God Is in the Small Details Too

Rhonda Rhoades
Joplin District

"Trust in the Lord with all your heart and lean not on
your own understanding; in all your ways submit to
him, and he will make your paths straight."
PROVERBS 3:5-6

"Look in the box," I heard the Spirit say as I walked past a moving box filled with blankets. We had just moved into a new parsonage and the box was in the church kitchen awaiting retrieval from the family who loaned us the blankets. I glanced at the box and saw it full of moving blankets. I kept walking. A few days later, I walked into the kitchen again and as I passed the box, I again heard the Spirit say, "Look in the box." Again, I glanced at the box of blankets and walked on.

We had moved on Memorial Day weekend, and a few days prior to the move, I had gone to my parents' home with our children. Jacob's birthday was right at this time, and my parents had given him a brand-new pair of Nike tennis shoes. I had seen them in the van when we arrived back in Garnett, but when Sunday morning rolled around and I was frantically looking for them, they were nowhere to be found. I was upset for two basic reasons. 1. Jacob desperately needed new shoes, and we couldn't afford them. 2. It was his birthday present from my parents! How could I lose them when I had just seen them two days earlier?

A few more days went by, and I walked through the church kitchen when I again heard the Spirit say to me, "look in the box!" So, this time I stopped and started removing all the blankets from the box. You know what I found, don't you! Yes, there in the box among the blankets were Jacob's new tennis shoes! I have no idea to this day how they came to be in the box with the blankets, but that didn't matter. What did matter was that God heard my prayers, my frantic, desperate prayers for those shoes.

In that moment, I realized that God was totally aware of my need and He answered my prayers. I was like the beggar sitting by the road who kept shouting, "Jesus, Son of David, have mercy on me!" (Mark 10:47). I kept praying for those shoes, and the enemy kept saying to me, "Be quiet. God doesn't care about a pair of tennis shoes, and besides, you're not important enough for Him to waste His time on." My "begging" in prayer resulted in me finding the shoes and learning a valuable lesson. God did care about a little boy and his shoes, and He cared about a mom who needed to know that what concerned her concerned Him.

Matthew 7:7 says "Ask and it will be given to you; seek and you will find; knock and the door will be opened to you." I had to ask for what I needed. We all do. There is no magic in asking, but ask we must. Asking reminds us WHO we depend on and who the answers are from. Even when the answer is "no," God can be depended on to give us the very best because He loves us the very best.

Years later, we fasted and prayed for this same child after he confessed sin to us. He was the one lost this time, not a simple pair of shoes. Again, God came through. I am committed to pray for the prodigals. God brought one of mine home, and I am joining with you to pray for yours. God answers prayer!

Prayer

Abba, we acknowledge that You direct our paths in the small and big things, and we say thank You. Now, O God, direct the paths of our children and grandchildren and open their ears to hear Your voice and their hearts to trust Your love. Direct their pathway to You. Amen.

He Stilled the Storm with Wit and Wisdom

Cheryl Roland
Northeastern Indiana District

"Be joyful in hope, patient in affliction, faithful in prayer."
ROMANS 12:12

We were at our wits' end. Have you been there? Psalm 107:23-27 describes a sailing crew who had come to their "wits' end" while staggering with fear and helplessness during a storm that threatened to snuff out their lives. We too were staggering under the stress and distress of a series of storms. My husband was consumed by a lawsuit a church filed against the district to declare their independence and ownership of property. Our daughter Kari, a freshman in college, lost her voice and for months was not able to speak above a whisper. And then, 16-year-old Cassie fell head over heels in love with a young man we soon learned was abusive.

The three crisis concerns were complicated further by the words of 1 Timothy 3:5: "If anyone does not know how to manage his own family, how can he take care of God's church?" We sought the Lord for assurance and cried out for wisdom, courage, and faith to stand strong. His loving response: "Don't give up!" (Romans 12:12).

God knew our sincere desire was to honor Him. Over time, the lawsuit was resolved and through that experience, we learned the great faithfulness of our Father who is a Rock we can stand upon. Kari's voice was restored. Through a miraculous answer to prayer, we discovered a voice clinic that specialized in her condition. In a multitude of ways, God has used her voice to sing, teach, and give Him glory as she encourages others to trust Him for physical healing.

And our good, good Father used Cassie's situation to humble us in His presence and teach us His ways. It was pride that kept us from sharing her struggle with praying grandparents and Christian friends. Ego not only prevents transparency; it also "edges God out." Once we died to self, it seemed we had divine direction. I called every prayer chain, prayer warrior, and TV preacher who offered to pray with us. We began praying with other parents whose children were making poor decisions. My husband contacted law enforcement officers for help in Cassie's protection. We invested in family counseling and were told we had a "missionary" who sincerely believed she had a mission to fulfill. I took her to the a shelter for abused women where she was taught the difference between healthy and unhealthy relationships. But ... she persisted, and they went off to Southern Nazarene University together.

It was there that Cassie experienced the loving concern of professors who not only contributed to her education but prayed for her and with her. I understand that some prodigals wait until they are old to return to the Lord (Proverbs 22:6). But for God's glory, I am happy to report that Cassie was healed in the strong name of Jesus! She married a godly man who adores her. She now serves as a school counselor, helping children make wise decisions and stand strong in the face of temptation.

The book *Parents with Broken Hearts* by William Coleman was extremely helpful. However, when we were at our very wits' end, it was God's Word that brought hope and peace. "He sent out His Word and healed them. He stilled the storm to a whisper; the waves of the sea were hushed ... and He guided them to their desired haven. Give thanks to the Lord for His unfailing love" (Psalm 107:20, 29, 30, 31). We are so thankful we didn't give up because at the end of our wit and wisdom was an all-wise GOD who taught us to trust, adjust, and obey.

Prayer

Oh Father, we love You so much! You are all powerful, all knowing, always abiding God. You are the God of all flesh. There isn't anything or anyone too hard for You. You are the glory and honor and power that cleanses us from doubt and fear. You rescue the perishing and still the storms to a whisper. We praise You, Lord Jesus. Amen!

The Good News Is for All

Debbie Scott
Sacramento District

"Honor God by accepting each other, as Christ has accepted you.
I tell you that Christ came as a servant of the Jews to show that
God has kept the promises he made to their famous ancestors.
Christ also came, so that the Gentiles would praise God for
being kind to them. It is just as the Scriptures say, 'I will tell the
nations about you, and I will sing praises to your name.'"
ROMANS 15:7-9 (CEV)

Stockton, California, is more diverse than New York City or Los Angeles. On January 23, 2020, Chelsea Shannon of ABC News 10 reported "Stockton, California has roughly 311,178 people who make up the most racially diverse city in America, according to the US World & News Report. The organization's study included cities with a population of 300,000 or more and ranked them by diversity. The data showed that Stockton has been pretty diverse in the ethnic breakdown of the population for several years."

I have lived in this great city for the past 27 years, but never in my wildest thoughts would I have believed Stockton is even more diverse than New York or Los Angeles. What an exciting challenge God has set before me! I am to be someone who belongs to Him, who shows His love on a daily basis to others who may or may not look like me.

One day my son came home from preschool. I knew when I picked him up something was amiss. He was very quiet the whole ride home. It wasn't long until I heard him in his room, digging in his tiny desk for his 64 box of crayons. I went on my way thinking he was about to work on his next beautiful, colorful creation. After a while, he made his way into the kitchen. "Son, do you want to help mommy cook dinner?" All of the sudden he thrust out his hand and exclaimed, "I'm NOT white!" He was holding the white crayon in his clenched fist. "Honey, who told you you were white?" He then went into a story about his best friend who told him he was white. "Mommy, we held our arms up next to each other and my arm is not the same color as his." My son still insisted he wasn't white. He held that crayon next to his arm and I had to agree he wasn't the color of that white crayon. I took him to his room and asked him to go through all 64 crayons to pick out which color he thought he was. I assured him he could discuss this with daddy as soon as he got home.

To this day, I wish I would have kept that crayon he picked. It was some obscure name I'll never remember. All I could think about was my four-year-old son was already dealing with being told he was different. We hadn't lived in Stockton very long, and I wanted him to feel like he was accepted, belonged, and loved.

Our Lord Jesus Christ longs for us to know that we are accepted, belong, and are loved. We honor Him by asking Him to forgive our sins and give Him complete control in our life. Once that personal relationship with Christ exists, it is then that we can accept, love, and make those around us feel like they belong. Maybe our Lord is bringing someone to your mind this very moment to reach out to. So many around us long to be included and accepted. We all have a desire to fit in and know that someone cares.

Prayer

Heavenly Father, I pray that You would increase my awareness of those around me that may be hurting. Help me to reach out often to our hurting world by saying hello and talking to my neighbors who are out on a walk, calling a friend I have not spoken to recently, or being a good listener and a kind face to anyone God brings my way. Lord, may I look in my crayon box of life and admire each and every person so they know they are accepted, belong, and are loved by me and more importantly by You, our Almighty Savior. Zephaniah 3:17 says, "The Lord your God wins victory after victory and is always with you. He celebrates and sings because of you, and he will refresh your life with his love" (CEV). In Your precious name, AMEN!

Unity through Prayer

Colleen Skinner
Rocky Mountain District

"I in them and you in me—so that they may be brought to
complete unity. Then the world will know that you sent
me and have loved them even as you have loved me."
JOHN 17:23

I grew up in a home with five children and wonderful, godly parents who nurtured us in the faith from our earliest moments. We knew we were prayed for every single day. I wanted that for the children I was hoping God would bless me with someday. My husband and I were students at NTS when we received confirmation that we were indeed expecting our very first child! My prayers immediately began to escalate!

The day finally arrived when we would actually see the face of the little one we had been so earnestly praying for. What joy! On our exit from the hospital, the hospital staff graciously gifted us with a car seat for our precious bundle. As we pulled away from the hospital, we were more nervous than we ever had been about driving. We were suddenly stricken with the realization that we had gently laid our little one into the car seat but never buckled him in! In our panic, we could have caused an accident right there!

We pulled over, both got out to help the poor child (like it would take TWO of us to click the buckle!), got back in our seats, and I broke down sobbing. The overwhelming reality came over me like a flood. We knew NOTHING about raising a tiny human being into healthy adulthood! Not only that, we knew nothing of what it meant to successfully pass our faith on to him and to raise him up in the love, fear, and grace of

Jesus! I began to understand why my mom and dad were so fervent in their prayers for us, often through tears.

This was the beginning of a lifelong journey for my husband and me as we grew in oneness through intercessory prayer for our children. That journey has only intensified as our children have grown.

It wasn't long before I realized how critical it was for me to also join arms with other moms and together intercede for our kids, watching God do what only He can do. I experienced the deep richness of being surrounded by moms of different nationalities and languages, praying with all their hearts, through tears, for MY children! I realized God was doing a deep work in my soul too as He shifted the load of their children straight into my heart. I began to pray through brokenness for their precious children as if they were my own. Together, we were carrying one another's burdens to the foot of the cross! Together, we were watching God do amazing things in our children's hearts! Together, we were seeing God's great grace being poured out in ways we could never have imagined. In the journey of praying together, a sweet bond of unity, peace, and love grows out of our oneness in Christ, filled with His Spirit! As we pray through the Scripture for our children, our faith is stretched and purified as we come to a deeper and deeper understanding of just how TRUE our God is to His Word! That oneness in Christ for all believers is the very thing Jesus passionately prayed for as He faced the cross.

Prayer

I pray that all of them may be one, Father, just as You are in me and I am in You. May they also be in us so that the world may believe that You have sent me.... that they may be one as we are one: I in them and You in me. May they be brought to complete unity to let the world know that You sent me and have loved them even as You have loved me (John 17:21-23).

Prayers That Matter

Rosie Smith
Iowa District

> "I urge, then, first of all, that petitions, prayers, intercession and thanksgiving be made for all people ... This is good, and pleases God our Savior, who wants all people to be saved and to come to a knowledge of the truth."
> 1 TIMOTHY 2:1, 3-4

One day I was visiting with my sister-in-law, and the conversation turned to the lives of our children and grandchildren. We are both very concerned for them and their decisions that will affect them spiritually, physically, socially, and financially.

Here are some points that I've been thinking about from a book I read recently. We can pray that our children

- be disciplined in their academic studies and lifestyle;

- grow in their relationship with Jesus and experience Him in His fullness;

- be aware of the enemy and his deception;

- have a hedge of God's protection around them so they will be kept safe physically, spiritually, and emotionally;

- will choose wisely and consider the character and lifestyle of the person each child chooses to date;

- will guard their hearts against sexual impurities;

- have an open and honest relationship with their parents;

- be careful who they associate with and choose friends who will have a positive influence;

- will have a hunger for God's Word to grow spiritually;

- will develop a good self-image but keep a good, balanced view of their beauty, charm, and strength.

As we all have influence in the lives of people, especially our families, we can have a sacred trust and an opportunity to influence their lives. As Esther stood in the gap for her people, we reflect our love for God and we share how He has blessed us in our walk with Him.

I need to be reminded to pray intentionally and deliberately and pray for their needs, hopes, dreams, frustrations, anxieties, fears, joys, and expectation. This will keep us on our toes (knees).

Prayer

Dear Lord Jesus, my words are so inadequate, but Your Holy Spirit is more. I ask in Your name to protect, encourage, and woo our children and grandchildren to Your heart. The enemy is seeking each one of them, to destroy the foundation of their faith. I know Your plan for them is better than anything this world has to offer. Please remind them of Your love and Your plan for them. For the ones that do not live close to us, I pray that someone will come into their life and lead them to the light of Your love and grace. Amen.

Worth the Wait

Debie Songer
Central California District

> "This is good, and pleases God our Savior, who wants all people
> to be saved and to come to a knowledge of the truth. For there
> is one God and one mediator between God and mankind,
> the man Christ Jesus, who gave himself as a ransom for all
> people. This has now been witnessed to at the proper time."
> 1 TIMOTHY 2:3-6

Mom was a preacher's kid, one of five who grew up loving God and married spouses with the same heart for Christ, except for one. My Aunt Elizabeth told me to never marry a man thinking you can change him, because she had done just that. She had been sure that she would lead Uncle Jay into a relationship with Christ, so she married him as he was—an unbeliever.

Every member of the family was praying for him. If asked about God's faithfulness and the power of prayer, every single one would say, "Absolutely!" And we faithfully prayed that Jay would be drawn to Christ. And as we prayed, months turned into years and years into decades. Jay's defiance toward Christianity was evidence to us all of God's gift of free choice.

Elizabeth and Jay's son, Dick, had just graduated from high school and was headed to college on two sports scholarships until that summer. On a family day at the lake, Dick was clowning around, diving into the waters dressed in a trench coat trying to capture the attention of all the girls. He eventually had everyone's attention, though not in the way he wanted. It took a little while for anyone to realize that he had not

158

moved in too long. It seems all 6'7" of him had landed on his head and his neck was broken exactly like Joni Erickson. This college-bound athlete was now a quadriplegic.

Dick, once an exceptional athlete, came to God through this experience and attended Nazarene Theological Seminary, where he became a chaplain.

He always said, "I can do anything anyone else can; I just go about it differently," and he did. My favorite of his sayings was, "I would rather be a quadriplegic for Christ than whole without Him." Many people came to Christ because of Dick's all-consuming faith in God.

You would think that seeing God's love through Dick's life would draw his dad into a life with Christ, yet decades passed and we saw no change of heart. As his wife and son became renowned speakers, telling others of the joy-filled life of faith in God, Jay remained unmoved. Even after spending two years living with emphysema, Jay stubbornly pushed away any God-centered conversations.

During one of Jay's hospitalizations, a simple country preacher met with him and Jay prayed, asking for forgiveness and beginning a new life in Christ. When he was asked why he accepted Christ when he did, his answer was, "I understood him."

We all rejoiced that day, wondering why he waited so long to accept Christ. Had relatives spoken in "church terms," assuming he understood, or pushed so hard that he decided to push back, or did he just like the conflict? Whatever the reason, the family had prayed faithfully, and Jay came into a relationship with Christ months before coming face-to-face with the One who had been calling him all along.

God desires that each of His creations, every person of every background, of every race, language, and degree of stubbornness join His family in the Kingdom of God eternally.

Prayer

Lord, thank You for choosing to be known by Your steadfast love. Please remind us to lift to You daily those who do not know You. Give us the faith to believe that You want a relationship with everyone You created and the wisdom to know when to speak, and more importantly, when to be still knowing that You are always at work, even when we cannot see it. Remind us often that Your Spirit is calling all to Yourself and You love each person more than we ever could. You are great and greatly to be praised and we trust You! Amen.

Trust in the Lord

Chuck Sunberg
General Superintendent Spouse

"Trust in the Lord with all your heart, and lean not on
your own understanding. In all your ways submit to
him, and he will make your paths straight."
PROVERBS 3:5-6

When I was growing up, my mother had "Christian stuff" all around the house: a picture in the kitchen of an old man praying over a loaf of bread; that famous head shot of Jesus; Precious Moments figurines sitting here and there; a family Bible on the coffee table in the living room and framed Bible verses hanging at strategic locations just so that we would not miss them. One hung over the toilet in the bathroom, about 18 inches above the tank. Needless to say, I noticed it a lot. Here is what it said: "Trust in the Lord with all your heart, and lean not on your own understanding. In all your ways submit to him, and he will make your paths straight" (Proverbs 3:5-6).

I remember coming home from high school one day all upset about something. My mother was ironing. I laid on her bed while she worked and I poured out my soul as she patiently listened. When I was finished, she looked up from her work and said, "Chuck, trust in the Lord…" She went through the whole passage while explaining how it related to my current situation.

I can remember calling my mom when I was in seminary, single and lonely, wondering if God had heard my prayers about someone to partner with me in life and ministry. She listened patiently then said, "Chuck, trust in the Lord…" Before too long, Carla came into my life. Mom was right again. I can remember calling to talk to my mom about many things along the way. She would pray with me and always say, "Chuck, trust in the Lord…" Those words got us through our years in Russia. We REALLY learned to trust in the Lord living there.

Our move from Russia back to America after 13 years was hard, especially for our two girls. They grew up in Russia. When we told them that we would be moving back home, they looked at us with tears streaming down their cheeks and said, "Home? This is home!" As soon as we got back "home," our oldest daughter went off to college. It would be her first experience with education in America. She was lost and it was very hard for her. When she would come home for a weekend, my little girl would sit in my lap and weep. I would hold her and beg God for the right words. Once in a while, I would hear my mom's voice saying, "Chuck, trust in the Lord…" I would say those words to my precious girl, hoping and praying that she was listening. She eventually finished college and moved to England to study theology. From time to time, we would FaceTime together and talk about life. Once in a while, I would say those words again, "Trust in the Lord…" hoping and praying that my mom was still right.

As the years have flown by, both my little girls have grown up, married great young men that we are eternally thankful for and, most importantly, they are giving us grandchildren that are the most precious little people in the whole world. Sometimes as I am sitting alone thinking about this and that, worrying about the crazy, mixed up, divided world that my grandchildren will grow up in, I hear my mom's voice. She is saying again, "Chuck, trust in the Lord…"

My mom was right! Well, it is more than that. God is faithful and true to His word. What is it that you need to trust God for today? Do you believe? Can you live right there? Trust in the Lord with ALL your heart! Don't look at what is weighing heavy on you these days only from your understanding. Your understanding is not complete. In all your ways, even when we are heavily burdened about something, acknowledge God. Turn your hearts to Him. Here is the promise for you today, He WILL direct your path. He will go with you and before you. I know because my mom told me. Not just that, I know because I have proven Him true; what He says He will do. Bless you, spouses! I thank God for you all!

Prayer

Father, we all need You so much. We are prone to lean on our own under-standing way too much. Help us all to lean on You. Help us to truly trust You with ALL our hearts and never look back. Pour out Your Spirit upon us as we seek to know You more and more each day. Amen!

A Song for Pilgrims

Debbie Taylor
Southern California District

"I lift up my eyes to the mountains—
where does my help come from?
My help comes from the LORD, the Maker of heaven and earth.
He will not let your foot slip—
he who watches over you will not slumber;
indeed, he who watches over Israel will neither slumber nor sleep.
The LORD watches over you—
the LORD is your shade at your right hand;
the sun will not harm you by day, nor the moon by night.
The LORD will keep you from all harm—
he will watch over your life;
the LORD will watch over your coming and
going both now and forevermore."

PSALM 121

As a young couple, we had always planned that I would be a stay-at-home mom until our children were school age. But early on, ministry changes required that I work outside the home, leaving my children in full-time child care. As a third generation PK, I knew I could trust God's direction. But as this reality began to set in, I must admit my spirit was greatly troubled. I couldn't understand how this would be the best for our children.

While Psalm 121:3-4 says "He will not let you stumble; the one who watches over you will not slumber. Indeed, he who watches over Israel never slumbers or sleeps..." (NLT), at times I found myself wondering if God was taking a "snoozer." Why is ministry costing me the privilege of watching my child take their "firsts"? Hadn't I always tried to be obedient and willing to do whatever asked of me? I was more than willing to give myself in whatever way asked, but not the raising of my children, Lord.

Upon arrival to one new assignment, many of the things promised and expected fell through. Our housing was compromised, our pay was half of the expected amount, and "safe" child care was not available. We depended on government commodities for food and grandma's temporary help babysitting. I remember thinking that we had made a HUGE mistake and feeling that God had abandoned us. We couldn't make our car payment, and on top of that, we felt God challenging us to make a Faith Promise commitment! My husband even preached a sermon: "When it seems nothing's happening, with God, something is always happening." Well, I thought He had lost it! This may be true in other situations but not this time.

In great despair, I cried out to the God of Psalm 121, trusting that my help would come from Him. And He answered as He always had! My job gave me a raise—the EXACT amount of the Faith Promise pledge! My husband called the loan company about our upcoming car payment to tell them that we couldn't make. We wanted to see if some adjustments could be made. The agent said, "Hold on a minute, Mr. Taylor." In a few minutes, he came back on and explained that there was a refund on our account from a canceled extended warranty (that we didn't remember doing). This refund would cover our payments for the next two months! Tom hung up the phone stunned! And the issue of childcare! Long story short, I ended up getting my child care license and taking in six kids plus my own two. It allowed me to not only look over the training of my own children but also provide godly care for others.

As a minister of music alongside my husband, I worried that too much church would not be the best thing for our family, but God used our family in dynamic ways, developing talents far beyond what I could have imagined. God led our children into areas of ministry of their own! And when the need for financial help for college came along, God provided a job for me as a public school teacher, allowing both our children to be able to graduate from Point Loma Nazarene University with no college bills! God proved Himself over and over again and taught lessons that would prevail for the remainder of our over 30+ years of ministry, testimonies of God's faithful provisions and protection to our family.

And now, as our children are building their own Christian homes and are confronted by challenges that could have never been anticipated, I can't imagine the God who has looked over them in the past will stop now. Verses 7-8 say, "The Lord keeps you from all harm and watches over your life. The Lord keeps watch over you as you come and go, both now and forever" (NLT).

Prayer

Dear Heavenly Father, as I continue to travel through this life, help me to keep hold of Your hand and trust Your promises, and sing as Fanny Crosby wrote: "All the way my Savior leads me; Oh, the fullness of this grace! Perfect rest to me is promised in my Father's blest embrace. When my spirit, clothed immortal, wings its flight to realms of day, This my song through endless ages: Jesus led me all the way!"[1] AMEN!

---

[1] Crosby, Fanny. "All the way my Savior leads me." www.hymnal.net/en/hymn/h/701.

We Are Our Children's Biggest Prayer Advocates

Angela Vassel
Metro New York District

"Perhaps my children have sinned and cursed God
in their hearts. This was Job's regular custom."
JOB 1:5b

Job was a righteous man who presented his seven children before God. He played the priestly role in the lives of his children. Job did not take anything for granted; he pre-empted any sinful engagement of his children while they were enjoying themselves. Job was concerned about the internal condition of their heart, the place that only God sees. Children of people in active ministry sometimes appear to be "saints" but are often resistant and resentful toward God in their hearts. We need to advocate for them. Job took his role in their lives seriously and was their regular prayer advocate. The description of Job indicated that he was a man who was not only preoccupied with living right himself but was also concerned for his children doing the same. Many of us pray much for the success and wellbeing of our kids but fall short regarding their relationship with their Heavenly Father. In addition to praying for them regularly, Job's prayer was specific for each of his children.

When our son was in college, he developed an interest in and engaged in illegal street car racing without our knowledge. He was not outwardly rebellious or disrespectful and was engaged in church but wanted to be a part of something that was validating among his peers. He had a car that was popular among young people, and he would spend his pocket money modifying the car with lightweight accessories. His car was stolen outside our house one night, and our son then shared with us about his engagement in this type of activity and some related, frightening experiences. We always prayed for our children bearing in mind that parents are not always aware of all that their children are involved in. We prayed specific prayers about things that were known and visible and general prayers covering areas that were not obvious. We are grateful that although we were not aware of this kind of activity, God knew and heard our ongoing prayers for his protection. God used the loss of his car to show him his folly and to open his eyes to other illegal activities that persons engaged in the street racing were involved in. He lost interest in this hobby and in acquiring any similar types of cars. My son is now a more mature and committed Christian and is a part of the staff at the church we last served. We saw God honoring His promises to us in Psalm 91 to protect our children He gave to us when we obeyed Him in answering the call to serve Him in the United States.

Prayer

Lord, I thank You for the blessings of the children and grandchildren of those who are Your specially assigned ministers. I pray specially for these children because of the challenges and burden they bear being pastors'/ministers' kids, which often leads to reckless behaviors. I pray for those that have been impacted negatively throughout the various ministry assignments of their parents and have become indifferent to the faith. I pray that they will realize that You love them with an everlasting love and that Your loving kindness will draw them to You.

Light

Natalie Ward
Global Missions Director Spouse

"In Him was life, and that life was the light of all mankind. The light
shines in the darkness, and the darkness has not overcome it."
JOHN 1:4-5

"Some people call this the 'Edge of Nowhere,' but we call it 'home,'
right, mom?!" This was a precious observation made by my young son
and one that rang true in my heart as well. Our missionary home was
nestled in the rugged mountains of Papua New Guinea. It was con-
structed of woven bamboo with a breathtaking view at 6,000 feet. The
nearest four-wheel drive road was days of hiking away. With no street
lights, porch lights, or any other form of electric light interfering, you
could literally put your hand in front of your face and not see it. This
made star gazing pretty spectacular! The people living in these mountains had captured our hearts, and we gladly called them friend and
neighbor. We thanked God for the opportunities He gave us to intro-
duce some of them to Him.

One night I heard my son calling out in the darkness. Something had
scared him and awoken him from his sleep. I made my way to his bed
with my flashlight in hand. After we talked a while, I reassured him that
"Jesus is with you, just ask Him to help you." He was thoughtful at this
point and really wanted to embrace my reassurance that Jesus is always
with him. Then he said, "Well, if Jesus is with me all the time, maybe
next time He could bring a flashlight!"

I smiled as I went back to bed, yet I was also thinking a bit more about
his comment. In the jungle, the darkness was something we had to
adjust to, plan for, and make our way carefully through. This was true

of spiritual darkness as well. I was challenged as I realized that I too ask God to "see" Him in very practical ways. I want to "see" His response to my prayers. I want to "see" light in the darkness that destroys.

Since that night, I have come to realize more and more that we sometimes do not "see" God, yet we can know that He is there! His presence can be very real and truly tangible. When we ask for light to be brought into the confusing and disorienting circumstances of life, He faithfully makes Himself known as the Light, and He is beautiful. May we lean into Jesus, who is the light of all people.

Prayer

Lord, may we be so much more aware of Your presence today, to be captivated by the light You are and the promise You give to be light in our lives. We want to know Your presence in the darkness we are experiencing—emotionally, physically, or spiritually. We trust You, Lord, with our loved ones and those You give us each day who know only darkness. May we be known as people of the light! In Jesus' name, amen.

Walk Like a Duck

Kim Willis
Philadelphia District

"My thoughts are nothing like your thoughts," says the Lord,
"and my ways are far beyond anything you could imagine."
ISAIAH 55:8 (NLT)

One late spring afternoon, I set out to take a social-distancing walk with a friend. I parked my car about a half-mile from a walking trail. We proceeded down the sidewalk toward our destination, casually talking and catching up. As we approached the entrance of the trail, we noticed movement on the sidewalk. As we came closer, we saw a mallard hen with eight babies walking in single file behind her. It looked like a little duck parade!

Unsure of the mother's destination, we stood still and watched. With great determination, she continued down the sidewalk while turning towards the street—a four-lane street, nonetheless. I know when God created this mallard hen, He placed within her a keen intuition to care for her ducklings and find a home for them near the water. However, I do not believe God gave her intricate intuition to maneuver traffic.

Bypassing our plans, we were determined to help momma duck on her journey. I walked on the edge of the highway at the front of the parade, and my friend walked behind. We came across several areas we felt might be a good home for the family to settle. She disagreed with our plans and even became agitated with us for trying to help. We had exhausted our resources, so we agreed to continue with her plan and simply guided them across the four lanes, hoping the traffic would cooperate.

As we crossed the highway, I spoke to my friend. "Isn't this just like the Lord! He has a plan for our lives; however, He allows us to go our own way. He is gracious and loving and often places others along our pathway to question our actions, warn us, guide us, speak wisdom into our lives, and in the situations we face, but ultimately, He leaves the choice to us."

Once the journey across the road was accomplished, the mallard hen led her young through the brush, onto some rocks, down an embankment, and into a beautiful pond that my friend and I didn't even know existed. As we watched this mother nudge her ducklings into the water and happily join them, I counted to make sure all eight were safely integrated into their new surroundings.

As we stood in awe of what we had witnessed over the past hour, God brought several things to my mind. The season we are living in has been full of changes and uncertainty. I am thankful for God's unwavering faithfulness.

"For the Lord will go before you, the God of Israel will be your rear guard." Isaiah 52:12

There were times during the experience when the mother duck would stop and all the ducks would lay down and rest. The road was long, the pavement was hot; nevertheless, when the trek was finished and they jumped from the rocks into the pond, it was obvious to us the trip had been worth the struggle.

"We must run the race that lies ahead of us and never give up. We must focus on Jesus, the source and goal of our faith." Hebrews 12:1b-2a (GW)

Prayer

Lord, help us to walk like a duck. In the name of Jesus, amen.

Huddle Up

Joy Wilson
General Secretary Spouse

"He ordered His angels to guard you wherever you go. If you
stumble, they'll catch you: Their job is to keep you from falling."
PSALM 91:11-12 (MSG)

The year 2020 had perhaps the most unusual "back to school time" any of us has ever seen. COVID-19 has dramatically changed our lives. If you have kids or grandkids in school, grown children, or school teachers in your family, they were all affected by the start of school, especially this year. Nothing looks the same.

One thing I remember most about the beginning of the school year while I was growing up is the "gathering around" we kids would do with Mom and Dad before heading out the door. Even on hectic mornings, time was made for a short "huddle up." The prayers we prayed helped us as we went to school. Some of our prayers were "May the words of my mouth and the meditations of my heart be pleasing in your sight, Oh Lord my Rock and my Redeemer" or "May the Lord watch between me and Thee while we are absent one from the other." When my husband and I had our own children, we continued those practices. We'd "huddle up" before sending them off to school.

I have drawn a lot of comfort from the verses in Psalm 91:11-12: "He ordered His Angels to guard you wherever you go. If you stumble, they'll catch you: Their job is to keep you from falling" (MSG). My favorite picture is a guardian angel watching over kids as they cross a bridge. Do you know the picture? I had one in my bedroom growing up. Not sure what happened to it along the way, but I soon found another one just like it and I still have it. It reminds me of God's care for our children and grandchildren, whether they are grown adults or still at home. I think of those children in the picture as MY children and grandkids and mentally see the arms of the Lord surrounding them. That visual brings me great comfort.

Today our adult children "huddle up" with their own children, our grandchildren. Our children, no matter the age, and our grandchildren, no matter how small, need our prayers.

Did you "huddle up" before leaving for school? What was your "huddling up" prayer? I am reminded that even though I'm not "huddling up" every morning physically with my kids or grandkids, I lift their names to the Father, the One who knows them best, the One to whom we dedicated them before they were born. We still lift them to Him every day!

Prayer

Our loving Father, thank You for loving us. Thank You that we can call on Your angels to guard and protect our children. Protect them physically and from the fears that afflict so many. Thank You for going before our children each day in what lies ahead for them. Give them wisdom to make wise choices, give them a kind heart in how they treat others, and a heart that wants to know You more and more. Amen.

Reconciliation

Joni Wyatt
Eastern Kentucky District

"All this is from God, who reconciled us to himself through
Christ and gave us the ministry of reconciliation: that God
was reconciling the world to himself in Christ, not counting
people's sins against them. And he has committed to us
the message of reconciliation. We are therefore Christ's
ambassadors, as though God were making his appeal through
us. We implore you on Christ's behalf: Be reconciled to God."

2 CORINTHIANS 5:18-20

Frustration, hurt, anger, broken trust, and polarizing factions lead to a fractured family; more specifically, MY fractured family. My beautiful family was once the "poster child" for the perfect pastor's family: my father and mother were the quintessential pastor and wife, and we four kids in tow were compliant (usually), uncomplaining (generally), and model PKs (mostly). We were a lovely, God-fearing portrait of near-perfection.

As the years rolled by and the world's darkness infiltrated our lives and families, we dealt with infidelity, deception, divorce, drugs, life-threatening illness, accidents, financial ruin, incarceration, and tragically, suicide. Finally, the journey through Alzheimer's with both parents simultaneously tarnished that happy family picture. God walked through it all with us. He was and is always, always there. But, for some reason, some of us have chosen not to be there for each other, to be ugly, unforgiving, and ungodly. We have siblings that refuse to talk, text, or have any communication with the others.

It's incredibly sad and disheartening to me. And I had begun to believe that it would always be that way. Then I was reminded of a beautiful truth—reconciliation.

As we attended our first church in the New Year, the pastor's wife gave a testimony and charge to choose a word to focus on instead of making lists of resolutions. God gave me the word—reconciliation. He reminded me that with Him, there is always hope of restoration, always a way back to healing, always forgiveness. As we are reconciled to God, we can be reconciled to each other.

I am trusting, praying, and choosing reconciliation for my fractured family this year.

Prayer

Dear Jesus, I am humbled and immeasurably grateful for the reminder that through You, forgiveness and healing are always possible. Thank You for strength, courage, and wisdom as I cling to You for each step of this journey. I pray I may live in Your never-ending faithfulness and in Your all-consuming love. And Jesus, I eagerly wait, ever-expectantly, in the hope of Your reconciliation. Amen.

Prayer and Intercession

Patty Warrick
General Superintendent Spouse

"Be still, and know that I am God."
PSALM 46:10

How many times are we really "still" in the presence of God? After dealing with several major surgeries, I found myself confined at home unable to do much. God definitely had my attention. He began to teach me some truths found in the above verse.

1. Be still and believe that what I have said in My Word is true.

2. Be still and trust Me to do what I have said I would do.

3. Be still and give thanks for what I have done, I am doing, and I will do.

4. Be still and wait expectantly.

Psalm 130:5 says "I wait for the Lord, I expectantly wait, and in His word do I hope" (AMP).

It seemed the Lord was saying to me:
Rest in His presence.
Rest in His promises.
Rest in His faithfulness.
Rest in His goodness.

May God give us the faith to believe and the patience to wait for answers. As God began to bring healing and to restore my strength, I became more convinced that my greatest calling is to be an intercessor. He gave these instructions to me:

1. I want to spend time alone with you. I want you to listen to Me. I have a work for you to do.

2. I want you to listen to My people. There are many who carry heavy burdens—health concerns, financial stress, issues related to children and grandchildren, aging parents, church-related matters—just to name a few.

   a. Point them to Me.

   b. Encourage them by sharing their burdens.

   c. Pray and intercede for them.

   d. Follow up with them.

   e. Leave My fingerprints everywhere you go.

I am learning that He has called and continues to call His people to be intercessors. Ezekiel 22:30 says "I looked for someone among them who would build up the wall and stand before me in the gap on behalf of the land, so I would not destroy it, but I found no one."

I am enlisting prayer partners—intercessors. We are all called to pray for others. We have no greater gift to give than to pray.

Prayer

May the God of peace fill you with His power and presence; may He enable you to become the intercessor He needs you to be for your family and your circle of influence. I pray this in Jesus' name and for His sake and for His Glory. Amen.

Prayers of Surrender is available in **print and ebook**
formats through major retailers. Find it in print at
amazon.com, walmart.com, and bookdepository.com.
Ebook versions are available through
Apple Books, Kindle, and Adobe Digital Editions.